"This inspiring and highly practical book will help you to find the courage to build a business from your authentic gifts so that you can serve the world by being you."

— **Rebecca Campbell**, best-selling author of *Light Is the New Black* and *Work Your Light Oracle Cards*

"This book is like sitting down with your best friend who tells you the unvarnished truth you need to hear, followed by the practical advice and loving kick in the pants you need to move forward."

— **Shelley Brander**, CEO of Knit Stars and *Wall Street Journal* best-selling author of *Move the Needle*

"The guide you need to turn your passions into a business that makes a lasting impact in the world."

— **Susie Moore**, author of *What If It Does Work Out?*

"Whether you're looking to create a side hustle or grow your current business, Market Your Genius *gives you a step-by-step process for consistently creating clients and customers."*

— **Lisa Sasevich**, best-selling author of *Meant for More*

"Nikki Nash takes the complicated and overwhelming world of marketing and makes it easy to understand and put into action, giving you what you need to turn your passions and talents into a company that makes an impact."

— **Emily Thompson**, author and host of *Being Boss* podcast

"An interactive discovery tool that brings the truest you and the business you want to build or grow clearly into focus with a proven step-by-step process for amplifying your message."

— **Nancy Levin**, author of *Setting Boundaries Will Set You Free*

"Market Your Genius *gives you the road map for packaging your much-needed wisdom into a profitable business. Highly recommended!"*

— **Kelly Notaras**, founder of KN Literary Arts and author of *The Book You Were Born to Write*

"A simple blueprint for creating a marketing plan that will help you build your audience while creating a community of raving fans in a way that is uniquely yours."

— **AJ Vaden**, CEO of Brand Builders Group

"Whether you are pivoting in business or starting anew, Market Your Genius *is an essential part of your entrepreneurial strategy."*

— **Shaunda Necole**, lifestyle influencer and creator of Pinterest Marketing Magic

*"*Market Your Genius *will ignite that fire within to go big with your dreams while taking you step by step through the process. Nikki provides what we all need to reach our goals as successful marketers of our unique genius."*

— **Tricia Brouk**, international award-winning director, producer, author, speaker, and founder of The Big Talk Academy

"A brilliant marketing mind who is masterful at taking the complexities of growing a successful business and distilling them into a simple, easy-to-follow blueprint that anyone can use to achieve lasting success."

— **Margy Feldhuhn**, CEO of Interview Connections

"If you're ready to turn your expertise into a profitable business, Market Your Genius *is your guide for getting there."*

— **Megan K. Harrison**, online course consultant and creator of Online Course Academy

"A step-by-step adventure in how to share your talents far and wide—and profit from them—without compromising who you truly are. It's a must-read for heart-centered, integrity-loving solopreneurs and small businesses who are ready to rise."

— **Annie P. Ruggles**, founder of The Non-Sleazy Sales Academy

"Nikki is a fresh voice in this industry who's written a book any entrepreneur could benefit from reading."

— **Tarzan Kay**, founder of Tarzan Kay Global and email marketing expert

"Through Nikki's expression of her real-life experiences and then her keen ability to draw the comparisons, I immediately realized that I need to spend more time in the 'dating phase' of my marketing attempts to get people excited about being in a relationship with me."

— **Keshia Butler-Thomas**, TV host of *Stop Surviving, Start Thriving* and CEO of Purposeful Life-Solution Focused Life Coaching

"If you've ever dreamed of turning your passion, skills, and gifts into a thriving business as a coach, speaker, author, or expert in an ever-changing world, this is the book that will take you there."

— **Megan Huber**, business growth strategist and co-founder of Structured Freedom, Inc.

"Market Your Genius *is not about focusing on what everyone else is doing to grow their business; it's about doubling down on your strengths and using what you've got to grow your business."*

— **Emily Merrell**, founder of Six Degrees Society

"Nikki Nash embraces the power of curiosity, simplicity, and passion—three key ingredients necessary for entrepreneurs who want to create more money and impact without the burnout traditionally known to come with those desired results."

— **Naketa Ren Thigpen**, balance and relationship advisor

"The blueprint for sharing your expertise with the world, creating a community of happy customers, and building a referrable brand."

— **Stacey Brown Randall**, award-winning author of *Generating Business Referrals without Asking*

"Nikki makes sure you not only own the genius you have to offer this world—but that you know how to monetize your change-making brilliance without selling your soul."

— **Coach Jennie**, author of *Hilda*

"Nikki shows you how to make the hobbies in your life marketable and turn them into consistent income."

— **Salisha Thomas**, Broadway actress and podcast host of *Black Hair in the Big Leagues*

"A must-read for high-achieving women entrepreneurs who need a marketing road map so they can step into their power as expert-preneurs and attract dream clients!"

— **Jessica Rhodes**, founder of Interview Connections

"With her straightforward storytelling and no-nonsense insights, Nikki Nash makes the complicated or overwhelming easy to understand and implement."

— **Dr. Erin Martin**, physician and international women's empowerment coach

"A must-read if you're ready to get more clients, be known as an expert in your field, and feel confident with marketing visibility."

— **Louiza Megan**, founder of Audacious Mothers

"Market Your Genius *takes the mystery out of marketing, offering a GPS for anyone thinking about taking the plunge into entrepreneurship or those stalling along the way."*

— **Nova Lorraine**, author of *Unleash Your Supernova*, founder of *Raine Magazine*, Pink Kangaru Podcast Network, and co-founder of The Raine School

"Building a business around your unique skill set is the future of entrepreneurship, and Market Your Genius *is the perfect guidebook to get you started."*

— **Shannon Siriano Greenwood**, founder of the Rebelle Community

MARKET YOUR GENIUS

HOW TO GENERATE NEW LEADS, GET DREAM CUSTOMERS, AND CREATE A LOYAL COMMUNITY

NIKKI NASH

HAY HOUSE, INC.
Carlsbad, California • New York City
London • Sydney • New Delhi

Published in the United States by: Hay House, Inc.: www.hayhouse.com® • ***Published in Australia by:*** Hay House Australia Pty. Ltd.: www.hayhouse.com.au • ***Published in the United Kingdom by:*** Hay House UK, Ltd.: www.hayhouse.co.uk • ***Published in India by:*** Hay House Publishers India: www.hayhouse.co.in

Cover design: Kathleen Lynch
Interior design: Julie Davison

The author of this book does not dispense business advice, only offers information of a general nature to help you in your quest for business success. This book is not designed to be a definitive guide or to take the place of advice from a qualified professional, and there is no guarantee that the methods suggested in this book will be successful, owing to the risk that is involved in business of almost any kind. Thus, neither the publisher nor the author assume liability for any losses that may be sustained by the use of the methods described in this book, and any such liability is hereby expressly disclaimed. In the event you use any of the information in this book for yourself, the author and the publisher assume no responsibility for your actions.

Cataloging-in-Publication Data is on file at the Library of Congress

Tradepaper ISBN: 978-1-4019-6155-8
E-book ISBN: 978-1-4019-6156-5
Audiobook ISBN: 978-1-4019-6289-0

10 9 8 7 6 5 4 3 2 1
1st edition, August 2021

Printed in the United States of America

To my loving parents and sister,
thank you for supporting me always.
Words cannot begin to express
the love I have for you.

CONTENTS

genius, noun:

1. exceptional intellectual or creative power or other natural ability.[1]

Everyone has it.

Gifts, talents, acquired knowledge, life experiences.

But a select few take their experiences and expertise and turn them into a profitable business.

Some call them experts.

Others call them gurus.

Entrepreneurs, Mentors, Coaches, Advisers, Consultants, Artists, Performers, Creatives, Influencers, Idols, Superheroes.

They have many names and many talents.

Some end up in the limelight.

Many remain unknown to the vast majority of the world.

But no one can take away their special gifts.

INTRODUCTION

"Owning who we are is power.
We've got to dare to stand out."

— Janet Mock, a kick-butt transgender rights activist who shares empowering stories as a writer, television host, director, and producer

On May 14, 2013, *The New York Times* published an op-ed written by Angelina Jolie entitled "My Medical Choice." The piece was about her decision to have preventive surgery. She inherited the BRCA I gene mutation, thus increasing her risk for breast cancer. I read that article while seated next to my sister, Ashley, in the back seat of my dad's car. My sister and I were both meeting with a geneticist to test for the BRCA II mutation. If we tested positive, we would be at a high risk for ovarian cancer.

This article couldn't have come at a better time. The month prior, my mom got her test results back. She tested positive for the BRCA II mutation. The same mutation that left my aunt Anita with an ovarian cancer diagnosis a few months before that; cancer claimed her life on December 3, 2015. The same mutation my grandmother Ruby had; she passed away of ovarian cancer days after I was born. The same gene mutation that I feared.

I had so many emotions that day.

What if I test positive? Should I have reconstructive surgery?

I'm almost 30, I'm single, what would this mean for the kids I want to have some day? Do I need to freeze my eggs?

I wanted to share with my closest friends what I was going through and how I was feeling, but I couldn't find the words.

When *The New York Times* published the op-ed, I had something I could share that explained what I was going through. It helped others understand what I was being tested for, why I was being tested, and what procedures I may have in the future. Jolie's experience made it easier for me to connect with my friends. Her experience made me feel as though I wasn't alone.

You have that same power within you.

Your stories, skills, and knowledge can make a profound difference in someone else's life.

All you have to do is share it.

One of the bravest things you can do in this world is share some of yourself with others. Your story has healing powers.

If you want to share your experiences and knowledge with the world, do it. I don't care how many times you've tried and failed before. It doesn't matter if everyone and their mother (including yours) thinks it's a terrible idea. And having disempowering thoughts and big-ass fears doesn't need to stop you.

If you want it, go all in. Commit to your dream and persist through the mistakes, roadblocks, and failures. If you want to be the person that goes after their dreams, show up as that person every day. And if you take a day off, don't let that day become decades.

Like you, I had a vision of making a difference in the world. And like many others, I delayed the dream for seemingly good reasons. After I learned that ovarian cancer ran in my family, I made the decision to start my own business.

I had a picture in my mind of writing books, speaking on stages, and even teaching others how to market themselves online.

I wanted to have more than enough money, to have freedom over my time, and to make a noticeable difference in the world.

To prepare, I started saving money from my paychecks, and in less than a year, I left my six-figure marketing job at Intel, hoping to make more money and an even bigger impact as an entrepreneur.

I'd like to say I started my business right then and there and lived happily ever after, but that's not my story.

Fear is deceptively powerful. It can sneak up on you, and you may not even realize it's there until it's too late.

On my last day at Intel, I had dinner with friends and finished cleaning out my townhouse. I wasn't just leaving Intel, I was also leaving Oregon. After a two-week detour in Puerto Vallarta, México, I was going to build my business across the country to be near my family in my birth state of New Jersey.

México was supposed to be my relaxation time before the entrepreneurial journey began.

Or so I thought.

The joy unfortunately only lasted a week.

Almost as quickly as the dream was born, fear creeped its way into the driver's seat.

What am I going to do for money?

Can I really make this work?

Can I really replace my salary?

Instead of sipping margaritas poolside, I spent the second half of my vacation glued to my laptop looking for another job.

I convinced myself that if I got a job at a start-up before launching my business, I'd learn how to build a business "the right way."

The truth is I chickened out of my big dream because I was afraid to fail. I was afraid that I'd look like an idiot for quitting a high-paying job only to fail as an entrepreneur.

Who was I to think that anyone gave a rat's behind about my story?

And anything I could offer already existed, right?

I thought more about failing than the possibility of succeeding.

Instead of leaving Intel to start a business, I took a head of marketing job at a tech start-up in Boston.

When going after your dreams, if you take a day off, don't let that day become decades.

I'm not sure how fear shows up for you, but for me, it likes to hide behind something rational.

Working at a start-up before creating my own business seemed like an excellent idea.

I moved to Boston for my new job and life seemed great.

Right up until it didn't.

Not because the job changed.

But because my desire to go after my dreams started screaming louder than my fear of failure.

In less than two years, I was back where I started. Quitting my job to start a business and unsure what my next steps should be.

All I had was that same dream.

The dream of writing books, speaking on stages, and having a business where I could help others create a life they were *MADLY* in love with.

A dream that only seemed possible for movie characters and the actors who played them.

Was this dream even possible?

After riding a volatile emotional and financial roller coaster for a couple of years, I discovered that the answer was *yes*.

Today, I own a training and development company that helps people turn their experiences and expertise into a profitable business.

I created a business where I'm making an impact in people's lives every day. And because of that, they are making an impact in someone else's life every day. The limitless ripple effect of my business provides me with an immense sense of fulfillment.

That being said, I made a ridiculous number of mistakes along the way. There were days and weeks that I generated five figures or more in revenue. Then there were months where I only brought in a few hundred dollars.

I put myself in what felt like crippling debt and had to take part-time jobs to supplement my income.

I felt shame, guilt, regret, and embarrassment all at the same time.

At one point, I realized that I completely lost confidence in my ability to make the business work.

I hit my entrepreneurial rock bottom. I owed so much money to credit card companies, my parents, and my once existing 401(k).

But while I thought debt was my biggest problem, it was merely a symptom. The real problem was that I didn't have the confidence to go all in on one marketing plan that could consistently generate revenue for my business, nor did I have the patience to validate it.

Inside this book, you will find a process for creating a marketing plan for your business and a system for validating it.

This book is for you if you:

- have an existing business as a coach, consultant, strategist, freelancer, creative, content creator, author, speaker, or service provider;
- are entertaining the idea of monetizing your stories, skills, or talents; or
- are somewhere between.

By the end of this book, you will have a customized marketing plan for generating new leads, getting dream customers, and creating a community of raving fans.

To help you achieve this, the book is divided into three main parts:

- How to **package your genius** in such a way that people want what you have to offer.
- How to **promote your genius** so you have a consistent flow of dream customers.
- How to **deliver your genius** so your customers continue to buy from you.

These sections will show you how to increase your business revenue, help more people, and build your reputation.

For more support, I've created a free companion course where you can find downloadable worksheets, marketing examples, interviews, links to additional resources, and supplemental videos. This chapter-by-chapter bonus material will help you enhance your reading experience.

Go to marketyourgeniusbook.com/stepone for access.

It should be noted that even with the best marketing plan in the world, you can still fail.

A plan on a piece of paper doesn't guarantee your business will succeed. You have to put the plan into action. This requires an unstoppable mindset and an accountability system.

You will see a noticeable difference in your revenue when you pair the systems in this book with an unstoppable mindset and accountability.

Inside the companion course, I also share a list of resources that have helped me take action despite my fear of failure and doubt. To access, head to marketyourgeniusbook.com/stepone.

To discover what will help you grow your business, you need to take action. Not just for your dream but for those who will benefit from you achieving it. While my sister and I tested negative for the BRCA II gene mutation, the entire experience inspired me to go after building a business. Like Jolie, your experiences and expertise can make a profound difference in someone else's life.

PART I

HOW TO PACKAGE YOUR GENIUS

In the "package" stage, you are distilling your expertise and life experiences into a solution to a problem. The goal of this phase is to get clear on the problem you are uniquely qualified to solve, identify who will pay for your solution, and design an irresistible offer that you will market and sell.

Chapter 1: Success on Your Terms. Before you jump into action, you need to know what you're trying to achieve. In this chapter, you'll:

- Clarify your company's purpose and vision so you focus on the right activities.
- Evaluate the status and health of your company so you know what is and what isn't working.
- Discover roadblocks you may face along the way so you can plan for potential obstacles.

Chapter 2: You're a Genius, Own It! To market your genius, you must first clarify what differentiates you from the competition. In this chapter, you'll:

- Identify turning points in your life so you can share your lessons with others.
- Uncover your superpowers so you know how to stand out in the marketplace.
- Choose what you want to be known for so you can build a name for yourself as the go-to industry expert.

Chapter 3: They've Got 99 Problems, but This Won't Be One. People buy products and services that they believe will solve a problem or realize a dream. In this chapter, you'll:

- Determine who would want to pay for your expertise and why so you can effectively market to them.
- Pinpoint the audience you should focus on first to get the biggest return on your investment.
- Learn what your target audience is thinking so your marketing resonates with them.

Chapter 4: The Path to Profitability. Once you know who will pay for your expertise, it's time to start helping them get results. In this chapter, you'll:

- Outline your signature product or next minimum viable offer so you can speak about your product with ease.
- Explore pricing strategies for your products and services.
- Discover how to land the first few customers of a new product or service.

CHAPTER 1

SUCCESS ON YOUR TERMS

"You cannot delegate vision."

— Beth Cross, business strategist, inventor, and horse lover who changed the equestrian footwear industry by applying technologies that were being used in other sports[2]

In high school, my aunt gave me the book *The 7 Habits of Highly Effective Teens*. In the book, Sean Covey, son of Stephen R. Covey, who wrote the book *The 7 Habits of Highly Effective People,* teaches teenagers the habits his father created for adults.[3]

Habit number two is "Begin with the end in mind." It's about looking forward and imagining what you want life to be. To be "successful," you have to know what success looks like for you.

A question I'm often asked is "What should I be doing to market my business?" To answer that question, you first need to know where you want your business to go. Then you need to know where you are right now. This way you can design a plan that will take you from point A (where you are) to point B (where you want to be).

This is no different than using GPS. You have to type in where you want to go for the system to map out a route from where you currently are. And if you have a fancy system, it will even tell you how to adjust your route when approaching traffic or setbacks.

In this chapter, you will get clear on what you want your business to look like, identify where you are right now, and discover potential roadblocks you may hit along your journey.

That's right! You have the fancy GPS.

IS EVERYONE IN BALI WITHOUT ME?

When I first started my business, I visited a networking organization called Business Network International (BNI) in downtown Boston. One of the members was building her online empire while traveling the world.

How the heck was she doing it? I wondered.

I scheduled a quick coffee chat with her and found that she was in an international group coaching program.

As a part of the program, she traveled with other female entrepreneurs to events around the world.

Each year the destinations were a little different, but over the years she had traveled to Paris, Florence, Miami, and Santa Monica, just to name a few.

As I researched coaching programs online, I discovered that people were building online businesses as international coaches, healers, stylists, mediums, speakers, authors, consultants, and course creators, all while traveling.

I read articles on Forbes.com and HuffPost.com about entrepreneurs who were making six and seven figures online.

I kept seeing Facebook and Instagram ads from people I'd never heard of promising the world: "build a business on your terms," "live the laptop lifestyle," and "make millions sharing your advice online." Every time I refreshed my feed, I saw entrepreneurs gallivanting in Tulum, Bali, Costa Rica, Paris, Dubai, Tuscany, and Maui.

I decided to do the same. At the end of my lease, I moved all my belongings from my Boston apartment into my parents' house in New Jersey. Their house became my home base while I traveled the world.

In just a few months, I traveled to places such as Spain, France, Norway, and Scotland. I visited old friends in Portland, Oregon, before heading to California and Hawaii. I was constantly in a new city, state, or country.

While I hit my goal of generating $100,000 in sales by the end of the year, I also racked up $40,000 in credit card debt. I blew through the $60,000 I had in stocks and inheritance. And since many of my sales were on payment plans, I barely had any cash in my bank account to kick off the next year.

I was focused on living a lifestyle that I ended up finding exhausting. Although I achieved my goal of traveling the world in style and being my own boss, I wasn't happy. And instead of thriving, my business was barely surviving.

As one of my first business coaches used to say, "You get what you focus on." I focused on traveling, and that's what I got. What I realized, however, was that I was focused on something I didn't truly want.

CREATING A CLEAR VISION FOR YOUR BUSINESS

Having a clear picture is essential to creating a strategy for your business. It not only helps you and your team know where you're going, it helps you make better decisions along the way.

As the visionary of your business, it is your job to take the picture out of your mind, put it down on paper, and share it with everyone who touches your business—even if you're a team of one.

Since your vision is the destination you and your team are trying to reach, it's important that you are clear and confident in the vision you create for your business. If you keep changing the destination, you may never get there.

The following pages highlight three exercises designed to help clarify your vision. These three exercises will help you answer the following questions:

1. Why does your business exist?
2. Where are you trying to go?
3. Who do you want on the team to make the vision a reality?

BLANK CANVAS

After I quit my tech start-up job, I sat on the floor of my apartment with a giant roll of paper spread out across the hardwood floor. I closed my eyes and visualized the world as I wanted to see it. Then I started to write and draw what I envisioned. When I was done, I began to think about the role I wanted my company to play in making that vision a reality. I then started to add to my initial picture, noting what I wanted my company to focus on and in what capacity.

The next day, I came back to the piece of paper. I looked at all the ways I wanted the company to impact the world, and I wrote each initiative on a separate piece of paper. I then asked myself the following three questions:

- Which initiative was I most passionate about?
- Which initiative did I have the experience and skills to start impacting?
- Which initiative could I focus on such that all the other initiatives were positively impacted?

The next day I looked at my notes and then answered a final question: Why does the company exist? I rewrote my answer every day for the next few weeks until I had one that I was happy with.

You can do a similar exercise to help answer the question "Why does my company exist?" I call it the Blank Canvas Exercise™. Knowing why your company exists helps you identify the reason you are investing time, energy, money, sweat, and tears into building a business. It goes beyond being your own boss and into building a legacy.

On days where you "just don't feel like it," it reminds you of the ripple effect you want to create in the world. The Blank Canvas Exercise helps you think big.

Here are some questions to ask yourself as you complete the exercise:

- What do you wish the world looked like?
- In the world you described, what are you most excited or passionate about?
- What skills, credentials, knowledge, stories, or experience do you have that could help make a difference in this world?
- Who are you passionate about supporting or helping in this world?

An electronic version of the Blank Canvas Exercise can be downloaded inside the free companion course. For access, head to marketyourgeniusbook.com/chapter1.

The Blank Canvas Exercise helps you identify your company's mission. It answers the question "Why do we exist?" Once you are clear on your company's why, it's time to create a vision for how your company will live up to its mission. That's where future forecasting comes in.

FUTURE FORECASTING

What do you want your business to look like in 10 years?

For many people, 10 years feels like a lifetime away. But 10 years can also fly by. Look at today's date. Then ask yourself what your life looked like 10 years ago? What has changed? What have you accomplished?

To help you clearly answer the question "What do you want your business to look like in 10 years?" you can do a future forecasting exercise. A future forecast can help you get clear on your company's local and global impact, financial goals, team size and culture, offerings, customers, and desired accomplishments and milestones.

Here's how to get started:

- Write a future date on the top of a piece of paper. This date can be anywhere from 3 to 10 years into the future. Next set a timer for five minutes and close your eyes. Pretend it's the date you wrote at the top of the page. Visualize what your business looks like.
- When the timer goes off, open your eyes and write a journal entry detailing what your business looks like on that date. Be as clear and descriptive as possible.

To reinforce your future forecast, read your journal entry every morning when you wake up and every night before you go to bed. Communicate the vision with your team by reading it to them regularly. This can be done at a monthly or quarterly meeting.

This exercise is designed to provide you with clarity on where you and your team are trying to go by a specific future date. Here are some prompts to help focus your journal entry:

- What impact has your company had on the world?
- What milestones has your business hit in the past [X] years?
- What products and services do you offer?
- What are your customers saying about you?
- How much revenue does your business generate annually?
- How many employees work for the company? How do they work together?
- What accomplishments are you most proud of?

Take time in the next few days to complete this exercise. Additional prompts and a video to help you create a detailed vision can be found inside the free companion course.

While the future forecast exercise helps you create the big long-term vision for your company, you can also do more specific vision exercises to get clear on how you will make that vision a reality. My personal favorite is the Dream Team Vision exercise.

DREAM TEAM VISION

Building a profitable business is rarely a one-person-does-all show. You will likely hire contract workers, part-time employees, full-time employees, or a combination at some point during your journey. This will bring a mix of personalities together, all working toward the same big vision.

Within my first year of business, I hired a virtual assistant (VA). Everyone I met seemed to have a VA so I thought I should do the same. I hired a virtual assistant my friend was using, and she was amazing. She understood the industry, had graphic design skills, and could write well. From a personality standpoint, we got along. But looking back, I hired her too soon. Not because my business wasn't ready for support—I needed the help and am grateful I had it—but because I didn't have a clear vision for what I wanted her to be responsible for or an onboarding process to help our relationship start smoothly.

The result was that I had an extra pair of hands scrambling to get things done in my business. I'd come up with ideas, and whatever I couldn't get done in time, I threw her way. When things didn't work out, I'd take a break from having a VA, only to get overwhelmed doing everything myself. I'd hire someone new and throw things to them, hoping everything would magically get done exactly the way I pictured in my head.

To hire a dream team and create a great place to work, you need to have a Dream Team Vision.

Like the future forecast, picture what your business will look like in the future, but this time focus exclusively on your team. Here are some prompts to help focus your journal entry:

- What team positions are filled?
- What metrics or results will each role be responsible for?
- What skills will each person need in order to excel at their job?
- How will people work together?
- What projects will you and your team be working on?
- What core values or attributes will each member of the team possess?
- Who will manage each team member to ensure they have all the support and resources they need to be successful?
- What systems or structures do you need to manage your team?

Your journal entry will help you gain clarity on the team you want to build and the way in which you will all work together. Once you have a clear picture, the final step is to answer the question "What type of leader do you need to be to successfully lead this dream team?" If you want to hire a dream team, you have to work on becoming a dream leader.

I wasn't prepared when I hired my first VA. I wasn't even prepared when I hired my second one. But after completing this exercise, I was prepared when I made new hires moving forward and created an environment where everyone could excel in their role.

To give you more support in hiring your dream team, inside the companion course I've created a Dream Team Toolkit so you can attract and manage your dream team.

YOUR STARTING POINT

Once you know where you are going, it's time to identify where you are.

Know that wherever you are in your business is neither good nor bad. It's just where you are.

Oftentimes when speaking with clients, my team and I will hear, "I feel like I should be further by now." I used to compare my results to what I saw on my Instagram feed. I believed that almost everyone was killin' it, except for me. I thought everyone was paying themselves multiple six figures and living their best life. But the truth is the 'Gram usually doesn't match industry statistics. Your journey is your journey. And no one can tell you where you "should be by now," not even your own mind.

Don't let someone else's highlight reel trick you into believing that's their daily norm.

In 2016, the International Coaching Federation published the average annual revenue for coaches.[4] Here are the results:

REGION	AVERAGE REVENUE
North America	$61,900
Latin America and the Caribbean	$27,100
Western Europe	$55,300
Eastern Europe	$18,400
Middle East and Africa	$35,900
Asia	$37,800
Oceania	$73,100

The study also shared that the global average was $51,000 in revenue. The key here is *revenue*. That doesn't take into account business expenses, taxes, or salary. In fact, it's unclear how many of the businesses were profitable.

You'll never have all the details of a stranger's business, no matter how transparent they are. When you focus on where you are and where you want to be, you can take the path that's right for you. This may or may not be the path of your favorite Instagram personality.

To help clients identify where they are, we have them complete an assessment. The intention of the assessment is to paint a clear picture of where they are right now so they can make informed decisions as they move forward.

On the next page you'll find an abridged version of this assessment. Complete it to get a better understanding of where you're starting from.

Take the time to slow down and get real with yourself on the current health of your business. This way, you can focus on actions that will make the biggest impact.

ABRIDGED BUSINESS ASSESSMENT

Remember, this is a judgment-free zone. The rating you give yourself is neither good nor bad—it just is.

Rate each category on a scale of 1 to 10, 10 being high.

1. **How clear is your company's purpose? ___________**

   Example of a 10: Everyone in the company is clear on our purpose and why we exist. They can clearly articulate our purpose in one sentence to a stranger.

2. **How clear is your company's vision? _______________**

   Example of a 10: Everyone in the company is clear on the three-year+ vision for the company and is helping the company realize that vision in their respective role.

3. **How defined are your company's core values? ________**

   Example of a 10: Everyone in the company is clear on our core values. They are not just words on a piece of paper; they represent who we strive to be every day and how we act.

4. **How much in demand are your products or services? ____________**

   Example of a 10: Our products and services are fully booked, sold out, or have a sizable waiting list. We're wildly in demand.

5. **How well do you know your target audience? __________**

   Example of a 10: We know our target audience better than their bestie. We know where they're spending their time, what they're thinking, what they're struggling with, what their dreams are, and so much more.

6. **How clear is your brand message? __________**

   Example of a 10: We can clearly articulate the results our customers and clients can expect or the value we bring in one sentence.

7. **How clear are you on your core offering? __________**

   Example of a 10: We could tell others about our core offering in one to two sentences.

8. **How confident are you that your clients will get results with your product or service? __________**

   Example of a 10: We have a page filled with testimonials and case studies of our customers sharing the results they got from our product or service.

9. **How well are you known in your industry or niche? __________**

   Example of a 10: We are the go-to expert in our industry. We are constantly interviewed on podcasts, asked to speak at events, and featured in the media.

10. **How well do you differentiate yourself in the marketplace? __________**

    Example of a 10: We have a signature system or process that has been trademarked or legally protected.

11. **How would you rank your marketing plan? __________**

    Example of a 10: We have a repeatable or automated plan that generates a consistent flow of qualified leads.

12. How would you rank your sales system? __________

Example of a 10: The people who get on the phone with the sales team or end up on our sales pages know they want to buy our product or service and can do so with ease.

13. How would you rank your referral system? _________

Example of a 10: We have a process that generates a consistent flow of referrals.

14. How would you rank your client retention system? _______

Example of a 10: Our customer lifetime value is above our industry's average.

15. How would you rank your mindset? _________

Example of a 10: My team and I do what we say we're going to do and have systems and support to combat inner critics or the inner excuse machine.

Remember, wherever you are is neither good nor bad; it just is. To track your progress, take this assessment every quarter and compare your results. For a downloadable copy of this assessment, head to marketyourgeniusbook.com/chapter1.

COMMON PITFALLS

Each chapter of this book is designed to aid you on your journey from where you are right now (point A) to the vision you created for your company (point B). Along the journey you may meet distractions or experience situations that take you off course.

In episode six of her podcast *Game Changers with Molly Fletcher,*[5] Molly interviews professional golfer Billy Horschel. During the episode, Billy shared how he visualizes himself being successful. He not only visualizes himself making birdies, holding the trophy, and conducting interviews, he also visualizes himself battling back from a bad start. Spending even 20 minutes a day visualizing helps Billy prove to his mind that he can accomplish his goals.

Over the years, my team and I have seen a number of clients before, during, or after they've veered off course. While there are a number of situations that derail people from their plan, below are the five most common pitfalls we've seen.

If you've experienced one or more of these pitfalls, know that you're not alone. In fact, I've fallen prey to each one of them. As you read these common pitfalls, take time to visualize yourself getting out of the challenge and continuing forward toward your vision. Like Billy, visualize yourself overcoming a poor start.

Pitfall #1: Spinning Faster Than a Chick in SoulCycle

When I started my business, I turned to a trusted friend who has yet to let me down. That friend is Google. If I wasn't working with a client, I was researching, trying to figure out what I should be doing and how I should be doing it.

I found a lot of advice.

A lot of conflicting advice.

Soon I found myself researching more than anything else. Researching to get more information. Then researching even more to validate the information I just found. I was spinning faster than a chick in SoulCycle down a path of confusion and overwhelm.

This vicious cycle of research, research, research cost me valuable time in building my business.

The world has no shortage of content. Between Google, YouTube, Instagram, Facebook, podcasts, and books, you can consume content every day for the rest of your life.

The problem is no one piece of content can give you the secret to making your specific business succeed. Yes, you can find road maps, guides, tips, and tricks. You can watch webinar after webinar or take course after course.

But acquiring more information through content consumption alone will not guarantee success. The only way to determine if the information you're consuming will work for you is by implementing it. And that goes for everything you read in this book.

The key is to quickly implement what you learn. Get in action. Put on your metaphorical safety goggles and run an experiment. Test that theory. Do the work.

Google is great. But if you spend your days behind the screen or with your nose in a book without putting any of the brilliant ideas into action, you won't have a business.

Knowledge is powerful. Just make sure you implement what you learn instead of keeping it all in your mind.

Pitfall #2: T.M.I.—Too Many Ideas

I love notebooks. It has been on my list to come up with my own collection of notebooks, journals, planners, and calendars for a long time. Putting ink to paper is one of my favorite ways to get ideas out of my head.

In my first year of business, I had an entire notebook filled with a beautiful game plan for creating a content marketing course, a group program, a one-day workshop, and a seminar.

I thought having a lot of ideas would be a blessing to my entrepreneurial career. But too many ideas can be a problem. If you've ever watched original episodes of the reality TV show *Project Runway*, you may have heard fashion mentor

Tim Gunn advises contestants to edit their work. In the show, fashion designers would compete for a six-figure grand prize by completing a sequence of fashion design challenges.

In season nine, designer Joshua McKinley became known for "overdesigning" his garments. He'd bedazzle the heck out of a dress, blazer, pair of pants, or skirt. He'd use feathers, beads, or anything sparkly he could get his hands on. Independently, his ideas were good. Together, they were sometimes a disaster. When Josh didn't edit out some of his ideas, he ended up with what the judges considered a "hot mess."

When you have a billion business ideas, you don't want to metaphorically put them all into the same garment. You'll want to edit, edit, edit.

When you don't, you end up confusing your target customer and slowing down the momentum in your business.

I've not only seen the curse of too many ideas be a problem in my own business but also with start-ups I've worked for, as well as with my coaching and consulting clients.

Until you've validated your first offer and know (1) that people want it, (2) that people are blissfully happy with it and will continue to buy it, and (3) that they will tell their friends about it, there is no reason to create a second product.

I've watched start-ups die because they tried to launch new products while their first product was consistently being returned and receiving one-star ratings.

Your products don't need to be 100 percent perfect before you create another one. Let's be real—that is pretty impossible. But it should be at a place where you have happy customers and a consistent lead generating system before you move on to the next one.

Pitfall #3: R.S.S. —Rapid Strategy Switching

The internet makes it easy for anyone with a computer to say their strategy is *the best way* for you to build your business.

Some people will tell you content is dead.

Others will tell you to build your business with content marketing.

Another person will tell you to go all in on speaking.

A different person will tell you that webinars are all the rage.

And let's not forget running ads and building your business on autopilot.

The opportunities for growing your business can seem endless. But for most people, they end up being a distraction. If you've ever jumped from strategy to strategy, you've experienced R.S.S.—Rapid Strategy Switching.

This happens when a person moves on to a new strategy or tactic before they've had time to validate the first one. There was a moment in my business where I suffered from R.S.S. I had three half-executed lead generation plans and nothing to show for it.

I had a webinar that I built and only delivered once. I had a 30-day challenge that I had mapped out 15 days before I decided not to continue. I even ran ads until I realized I wasn't getting the return on investment that I wanted and moved on.

The reality is that any of these activities could have worked for my business. But I didn't give any of them enough time or attention to know for sure.

Pitfall #4: Inconsistent Marketing

There have been days that I just didn't feel like coming up with another Instagram post or writing another email to my list. Some days I'd push through and do it anyway, and on others, I let my feelings run the show. If you've ever stopped all marketing until you "figure it out" or "have more time," you too have visited the inconsistent marketing camp.

Inconsistency adds friction to the momentum you are trying to build in your business.

I've done it more than once. I've stopped posting on Facebook because it became "exhausting to go live." I stopped running ads because I "wasn't sure if it was working." I gave up seeking referrals because I "didn't want to bother people."

Your business will not succeed if it runs according to your feelings.

If the action you're taking isn't yielding the results you want, tweak what you're doing and analyze the results.

Consistent action can be tweaked so it's the right action. When you stop altogether, you miss out on valuable data and information.

I bet there are things in your life that you do consistently. Think about what helps you stay consistent with those activities. Then see if you can put a similar structure or mindset in place to be consistent with your marketing. For example, I know I'll get things done when someone else is relying on me. When I started the *Market Your Genius* podcast, I struggled for about a month to consistently release content. But after hiring an editor and empowering him to hold me accountable for being on time, I've never missed an episode. In fact, he's never had to call me out for being late with my episodes. Knowing that he needs them was the motivation I needed to stay consistent with the show.

Pitfall #5: Unvalidated Marketing

Have you ever felt like all your marketing efforts do not match your revenue or business growth? Know that you are not alone. This is one of the biggest frustrations I hear from entrepreneurs. Unvalidated marketing is often the culprit.

Validated marketing means you have a system in place to know if your marketing plan is working and can pinpoint where your plan is falling short. Marketing is just one giant science experiment, and your job is to prove your plan (or hypothesis) works.

That means you need to create and test your marketing plan over and over again. If you've ever felt that "nothing's working to grow your business" or that you've "tried everything," I recommend that you create one marketing plan and execute the plan consistently for a year. Look at your metrics weekly and make small tweaks and adjustments to your plan until you are getting desirable results.

Take the time to create and validate a plan that will yield consistent and predictable results. I go into this in more detail in Chapters 5 through 8.

IMPLEMENTATION CHECKLIST

The goal of this chapter is to help you get clear on why your company exists, define where you're going so you and your team can all move toward the same goals, and give you an idea of some potential roadblocks you'll meet along the way. Remember, wherever you are right now is neither good nor bad; it just is. And having the clarity of knowing where you want to go and where you are now will help you create a pathway to achieve your definition of success.

If you haven't already, complete the exercises from this chapter before you move on to the next. Use the following checklist to keep track of the exercises you complete.

- [ ] Get clear on why your business exists with the Blank Canvas Exercise.
- [ ] Ensure you and your team are working toward the same outcome with a Future Forecast Exercise.

- ❑ Paint a clear picture of the team you desire to have and how you'll work together with the Dream Team Exercise.
- ❑ Identify where your company is right now so you can build a plan that gets you to your big vision by completing the Abridged Business Assessment.
- ❑ Access electronic versions of each exercise and additional resources by heading to marketyourgeniusbook.com/chapter1.

In the next chapter, you'll get guidance on choosing what you want to be known for so you can start sharing your stories and skills with the people who will want to buy from you.

CHAPTER 2

YOU'RE A GENIUS, OWN IT!

"Energy rightly applied and directed will accomplish anything."

— Nellie Bly, a "go all in" 20th-century journalist who faked insanity to expose the poor treatment of individuals in asylums

One of my first clients "Nadia" had a drool-worthy background in finance. She worked at some of the top financial institutions in the U.S. Knowing she wanted to start her own business, she decided to build a financial advisory firm for female entrepreneurs.

Throughout our sessions I could tell something was stopping her from going all in with her business. Week after week, I would give her assignments. And week after week she had reasons for not taking action.

There are plenty of things in this world you can do to make yourself miserable; don't let starting a business be one of them.

After a couple of weeks, I asked if she was excited about building this business. Almost immediately she started to cry.

"I want to have a business so badly! I just don't want to spend my days in finance anymore."

You get to choose what business you create. Don't build a business you're not excited about or spend your days positioning yourself as an expert in something solely because you have an extensive background in it.

While Nadia had financial knowledge, she also had experience navigating corporate America, building highly efficient teams, and effectively creating boundaries so she could focus on what was important to her. Instead of building a financial advisory firm, she built a life coaching business focused on overextended working women. She taught the systems and structures she used to get promoted to SVP in her company while meeting her partner, getting married, and having three children without burning out. She felt passionate about helping women create boundaries so they could experience more freedom.

I've had clients with backgrounds in accounting build life coaching businesses. I've seen marketers become photographers, lawyers become health coaches, and teachers become mindset coaches. The list goes on.

Creating a fulfilling personal brand business means finding the intersection between your passions and your expertise.

BUT I'M NOT AN EXPERT!

Being an expert is a lot simpler than many people imagine. Unless it's a mandate for your industry, it does not require a certification or a license. It simply requires that you've done something over and over until you are really good at it, if not better than most. For example, you may have an apple cake recipe you've perfected over time. Your children love the cake and friends rave about it at parties. In a financial bind, you decide to sell the cakes. If you could just sell 100, you'd be in good shape. Within a few days, you sell 42. Momentum continues to build. Your initial idea of selling 100 apple cakes to pay past-due bills suddenly becomes a thriving business. This is absolutely possible for you. In fact, it's the real story of former model and actress Angela Logan, who started selling apple cakes to get out of foreclosure.[6] Mortgage Apple Cakes was created because Logan monetized an expertise that she had, even though she had never been paid for it before.

Your job is to identify what you want to be known for and, if it excites you, turn it into a profitable business. To help you find clarity, we'll explore the following four categories:

1. Your Experiences (stories)
2. Your Expertise (skills, knowledge, etc.)
3. Your Superpowers (natural abilities, personality, unfair advantages, etc.)
4. Your Interests (passions, desires, etc.)

EXPERIENCES

I bet you have had experiences where your insights from it could impact a stranger's life. These experiences may have changed the trajectory of your life, changed the way you see the world, or given you an epiphany that has shaped decisions you have made throughout life.

For me, finding out that the BRCA II mutation ran in my family made me realize that life was too precious to spend it in a career that didn't fulfill me. It was the reminder I needed at that point in my life to stop going through life like a soulless zombie and start creating a life I was *MADLY* in love with.

Here are some prompts to help you brainstorm experiences:

- Think about at least three moments that were turning points in your life.
- What situations have left you believing "this happened for a reason"?
- What have you learned about love?
- What have you learned about life?
- What have you learned about money?
- What have you learned about health?
- If you could go back in time and teach your younger self five lessons, what would they be and why? What experiences led you to want to share these lessons with your younger self?

EXPERTISE

Even though I created Intel's Instagram account and co-created their Pinterest account, I didn't consider myself an expert. But my boss suggested I share my social media knowledge to other members of our department. Determined to show my boss that I could help raise the social media IQ of the North America marketing team, I started a monthly lunch-and-learn series called Getting Social with Nikki. In each session, I'd choose one social media platform and do an in-depth training on it before opening the meeting up for questions.

To prep each month, I did extensive research and tested what I learned. I wanted to make sure that if anyone asked me a question, I either knew the answer or knew exactly where the answer could be found.

With each Getting Social event, I felt more like a social media expert. It was from this experience that I realized other people saw me as an expert before I did. The same could be true for you.

To uncover your expertise, answer the following questions:

- What topics do people ask you questions about?
- If you asked your friends, family, or colleagues what your expertise is, what would they say?
- What could you confidently teach someone else how to do?
- When have you witnessed someone struggling to solve a problem and you thought to yourself, *I've got this*?
- What results have you helped someone else achieve?
- If you had to do a 60-minute workshop five minutes from now, what would you be able to talk about with ease?
- What have you accomplished in your lifetime?
- What topics do you have extensive knowledge on?
- If someone paid you to write a book teaching something without referring to books or the internet, what could you write about?
- What skills have you developed over time?

Try not to edit yourself during the process. The answers don't have to be related to a specific task, activity, or subject matter. Simply write down everything that comes to your mind.

SUPERPOWERS

One day, a few years after graduating from college, I was sitting on a bench at the Summit, New Jersey, station waiting for a train to New York City. I was reading a really good book when a woman, who was about 15 years older than me, started talking to me about her life. I learned about her career, her experience at Columbia where she earned her MBA, and her family. At the end of our conversation, she even agreed to help me with my MBA applications, which she, in fact, did months later. Many of my friends found this weird, but it wasn't the first time something like this happened to me and it won't be the last.

In fact, I distinctly remember sitting on a packed Amtrak train a few years later when a guy around my age sat next to me and told me his entire life story, including his relationship with his girlfriend and his experience building a business.

For some reason, without doing anything, people feel compelled to share their life with me. In high school, I was often the person who knew everyone's secrets. Not because I sought them out, but because people felt comfortable talking to me about what they were going through.

As I got older, I kept hearing the same phrases from strangers. The two I heard most were "Wow, you are easy to talk to" and "You have great energy."

I do not know if this is something I was born with or developed over time, but I consider one of my superpowers to be the ability to make people feel comfortable and safe without saying a word.

There may be a million other people who "do what you do." But there is only one you.

There are things you're naturally good at and seem to be a part of who you are. While you may not see how it could be a business, identifying your superpowers can help you get clear on what you want to be known for and what differentiates you from competitors.

To start identifying your superpowers, answer the following questions:

- What things come easily to you?
- What do your friends and family say you're naturally good at?
- What do people seek you out for?
- What do people often say about you or to you?

Your list may inspire a business idea or simply be a characteristic of your brand that sets you apart from the competition.

INTERESTS

Like Nadia, the financial adviser turned life coach, you can build a business in an industry you haven't had a career in.

One of my clients, "Sabrina,"did just that. She was interested in why some people took action toward what they wanted and why other people seemed stuck. She wanted to help people get out of the metaphorical mudhole they were in and pull themselves out. Her background was in marketing, not psychology, neurology, or human behavior. But she was passionate about and interested in the topic, so she committed to getting trained. She completed certification programs, read books, attended seminars, and took courses. She applied everything she learned to her own life then started working with clients.

Some of you may be interested in topics or industries that are directly related to your life experiences and area of expertise. For others, you may have areas of interest that you wish you could start a business in even though it's different from the career you've had. This is no different than deciding on a career change. There will be skills that are transferable, but you'll need to get trained and learn the new industry firsthand.

Below is a list of questions to help you identify areas that you are interested in building a brand around.

- What topics would you be excited to talk about for the next three to five years?
- What topics would you love to teach others about?
- Pretend you've just been asked to do a segment on the *Today Show*. What topic do you see yourself talking about?
- You're about to do a book tour for your first book. What is that book about?
- You have been asked to give a workshop on the same topic for the next 12 to 18 months. You're superexcited that the workshop is about ________________.

IF MATTHEW MCCONAUGHEY CAN DO IT, SO CAN YOU

Do you remember your first Matthew McConaughey movie?

Was it *The Wedding Planner, How to Lose a Guy in 10 Days,* or *Failure to Launch*? Or did you first see McConaughey in *Dazed and Confused*?

While I can't remember exactly when I decided it would be amazing to have Matthew McConaughey in my friendship circle, I do remember watching *How to Lose a Guy in 10 Days* every time it came on television.

I love a good Matthew McConaughey romantic comedy, but something magical happened around 2013. In 2013, I discovered that I loved Matthew McConaughey in dramas.

Dallas Buyers Club, The Wolf of Wall Street, True Detective, I love them all.

In what felt like a blink of an eye, McConaughey transitioned from being known for romantic comedies to being a star in dramas.

The only box you're ever in is the one you put around yourself.

So what does Matthew McConaughey's acting career have to do with your business?

Whatever you decide your niche to be, know that it doesn't need to be the only thing you or your business will be known for until the end of time.

Like Matthew McConaughey, you can shift genres.

Will Smith went from comedy to action to drama. And let's not forget his rapping career.

Nicole Richie went from reality TV to fashion designer and author.

Charlize Theron went from being a model to playing serial killer Aileen Wuornos and winning an Academy Award for Best Actress in a Leading Role.

Laurence Fishburne was Cowboy Curtis on *Pee Wee's Playhouse* way before he was Morpheus in *The Matrix*.

Oprah Winfrey went from being a news anchor (a job she was fired from for being too "emotive while giving the news") to a media executive, actress, producer, and billionaire.

The list goes on.

This means that whatever you choose your niche to be, it doesn't mean you have to stick with it forever if you don't want to.

You don't have to do the same thing forever. Create a business you believe you can build for the next 5 to 10 years. If and when you decide to expand your niche or launch an entirely new business, go for it.

If you want your business to succeed right now, pick one thing you can get behind and focus on. Leverage it to build your audience and make a name for yourself.

IMPLEMENTATION CHECKLIST

The goal of this chapter is to help you get clear on what you want to be known for. This will be the lens through which you build, grow, and scale your business. It's what will differentiate you from competitors.

Before jumping into the next chapter, use the checklist below to make sure you're implementing what you've just learned.

- ❑ Journal about your future business. Highlight what you'll speak about on stages, what you'll write books about, and what you'll be known for.
- ❑ Review your stories, skills, superpowers, and passions, then choose the one main topic you would like to be known for over the next three to five years.
- ❑ Access electronic versions of each exercise by registering for the free companion course. Head to marketyourgeniusbook.com/chapter2 for access.

In the next chapter, you'll get guidance on identifying your target audience. In order to market and sell your products, you'll need to understand who would want to buy your products and services and why.

CHAPTER 3

THEY'VE GOT 99 PROBLEMS, BUT THIS WON'T BE ONE

"One of the more powerful outbreaks of happiness and meaning in your life will occur when you pair your passion and the world's need."

— Sue Monk Kidd, registered nurse turned best-selling novelist of *The Secret Life of Bees,* who announced to her husband on her 30th birthday that she was going to become a writer[7]

When I was in middle school, I volunteered at a nursing home. During one of my visits, I met a woman who had a hobby of painting small boxes. These boxes could fit earrings, rings, or other small objects.

One day during a visit, she mentioned that she had a lot of boxes and wasn't sure what she would do with them. I offered to sell her boxes, and she sent me home with a ton of them. I was so excited to help her. I loved these boxes and truly believed they would be easy to sell. After all, who could resist buying a beautiful box from a middle schooler who was selling them on behalf of an elderly lady?

Apparently, a lot of people could resist the urge. I didn't sell one box. Not one. I'm pretty sure these boxes are still somewhere in my parent's basement.

I'd like to say I learned a valuable lesson about business back then, but I was about 11 and, honestly, I just felt crushed.

THANKS, BUT NO THANKS

When I tried to sell those decorative boxes, I did not realize the importance of market demand.

I simply had an idea I believed in and went for it.

Did people even want these decorative boxes?

I had no idea.

This is not a unique situation either.

Research by CB Insights found that 42 percent of start-ups failed due to "no market need."[8]

While the demise of a business is rarely due to one single factor, you need demand for your product or service for your business to work.

If your business is not, at its core, delivering something people want and are willing to pay for, you are setting yourself up for failure.

When I started my first business, I was guilty of what many first-time entrepreneurs do. I started working on an idea before determining if the idea would be profitable.

In an era when people can start a business with an internet connection and a bank account, it's important to investigate if your business idea is viable. Otherwise, you could be left with an expensive hobby or a basement full of decorative boxes.

To build a business from your genius, you must identify where your expertise is wanted and if someone would pay enough for you to make a profit. The question you are trying to answer is "Who has the problem I can solve and is willing to invest in solving it?"

If you have a desire to help people transform their money mindset because you once had a terrible relationship with money and transformed it for a better life, that's great.

If you want to start a business doing that, it would be a good idea to first identify the people who want to transform their relationship with money and determine if they will pay for the help you can provide. Whether you've been in business three minutes or three years, if you haven't evaluated if your business has enough demand for the long haul, take the time to do so.

How do you determine if your idea can become a profitable business? Here are six areas to consider:

1. You've Got It, They Want It

I once worked for a company that created a baby monitor that tracked a baby's breathing. It would alert the parent if there was an anomaly. Was this for every parent? No. But it sold particularly well with parents of preemies and parents who were concerned about sudden infant death syndrome (SIDS). When you have an idea for a business, ask yourself "Who would want this?" Write a list of all of the groups of people who would buy your products then get to know them better. For the baby company I worked for, we spoke to new parents, parents with preemies, and parents who were tech enthusiasts. We held small focus groups to understand if and why they'd want our product.

You do not need to be right for everyone, just for enough people to make financial sense.

2. Cash or Credit

Finding people who want what you've got is only part of the puzzle. They not only have to want it, but they have to be willing to pay enough for it so you make a profit. Clients often come to me saying they want to help a certain target audience because they need what they are selling. People needing your products or services is not a prerequisite to profitability. For your business to work, you have to consider where the money will come from. I'm not saying you have to start a business for the money or sell your soul just for profit. I'm simply saying that you must think about where the money will come from so you can pay yourself and continue to grow your business.

Not all business models require the end user to have the money. Maybe you're paid by insurance companies. Maybe your business receives grant money from the government or through fundraising events. Maybe you make money through corporate sponsorships or advertising.

The question you must ask yourself is "Who will pay for what you're selling so it makes a profit?"

3. One-Time Sale or Repeat Business

Growing up, there were kids who lived up the street that would shovel our driveway and walkway every time it snowed. It felt as though the second there was a snowflake falling from the sky, they were knocking on the door to see if my parents wanted their services again. I have no idea how much money these kids made, but I do know they had a consistent flow of customers every winter.

I have had tons of business ideas over the years, but one thing I look at is the potential lifetime value of a customer. A customer's lifetime value (CLV) is how much revenue a customer is predicted to spend with you during their lifetime.

If you are building a lemonade stand in your driveway on a quiet street where people rarely walk around the neighborhood, you may only have one-time customers. If you're selling a cup of lemonade for $0.99, then their CLV is $0.99.

However, if you set up a coffee shop in a high-traffic area, sell an assortment of foods and beverages, create a space for people to meet and chat, plus offer a frequent buyer rewards program, you have Starbucks, for which in 2016, KISSmetrics estimated their average CLV to be over $14,000.[9]

Ask yourself, "Will your business idea have longtime customers?"

4. One-Hit Wonder

Do you remember when Trolls dolls were a thing? If you have no idea what Trolls dolls are, they were figurine trolls that came in different colors and had hair that stood straight up. They were created in 1959 and went in and out of style for decades,[10] becoming a big thing again in the 1990s. Most kids in the U.S. either had one or wanted one, myself included.

If in the '90s someone told me I could make bank by either selling Trolls dolls or making and selling accessories for Trolls dolls, I would have believed them.

But guess what? Trolls dolls didn't stay in high demand. You could have a brilliant business idea, but you have to ask yourself, "Will this idea have longevity or is it just a fad?"

An industry that frequently has new fads is health and wellness. Tae Bo, P90X, Zumba, CrossFit, Keto, Atkins, Zone dieting, the list goes on. Can you build a business by attaching yourself to what's on trend? Sure. The question you have to ask yourself is "Will the market keep generating new clients for me to service, or is this a trendy business opportunity that will fade out?"

5. Problem Solved, Dream Realized

People buy products and services for several reasons. Solving a problem, achieving a big dream, aspiring to be seen a certain way, and being a part of a community are at the top of the list. When you are turning your experiences and expertise into a business, you're most likely helping people solve a problem so they can achieve a big dream.

When you evaluate the market opportunity for your business, it's important to identify the problem you're solving and understand how urgent it is for your target market to solve that problem.

If you're a book coach and you ask someone if they want to write a book and they say yes, you might be under the impression that they are your target customer. But they may not be. Lots of people want to write books, but most people won't. Try not to mistake people's belief that your offering would be "nice to have" with being an "absolute must." If that same book coach spoke to a business owner who needed to position themselves as an expert in the market and strongly believed that writing a book now would have a profound difference on their bottom line but didn't know where to start, that's a much stronger target customer.

Ask yourself if there is a target market that will prioritize buying what you offer or if it is a "nice to have" for everyone.

6. A Competitor at Every Turn

Before I started my business, I could count the number of coaches I knew on one hand. The one executive coach I knew of was through a leadership development program at Intel that helped potential future leaders grow and develop so they could rise up the ranks. She was the first coach I worked with who wasn't in athletics. Years later, when I launched my business full-time, I discovered that the coaching and consulting industry had been rapidly growing.

Knowing there is demand for your products and services is just one part of the equation. It's also important to understand the industry in which you are building your business. How saturated is your market?

In *Blue Ocean Strategy: How to Create Uncontested Market Space and Make the Competition Irrelevant,* authors Renée Mauborgne and W. Chan Kim[11] discuss creating and capitalizing from an uncontested marketplace. If you're metaphorically the only business in a big blue ocean, there is no competition.

One company that comes to mind is Netflix. Not only did they disrupt the video rental industry, they established an entirely new marketplace for streaming content.

That being said, having a business idea in a saturated market doesn't necessarily mean you shouldn't start your business. If the market you're interested in has a lot of competition, you should (1) evaluate how well the competition is doing and (2) have a plan for differentiating yourself. A competitive marketplace could be an indicator of high demand. The key is to identify if there is enough demand for you and if there's an opportunity for you to differentiate yourself such that you either take some of the market share or attract an entirely new audience to the industry. Ultimately, your goal is to answer the question, "Can I build a profitable business?"

KEEP IT SIMPLE, SISTA

Doing some market research before you launch your business or your next product doesn't need to be complicated. Start by being curious.

Speak to as many people as you possibly can to understand what they need and want.

Be so curious that you are open to discovering a business opportunity you never would have imagined.

Let's say you started your quest with the desire to be a money mindset coach. But after conducting market research, you discovered another opportunity. Instead of being a coach for adults, you decide to become a curriculum consultant specializing in teaching money management to young children at private and charter schools.

Market research can help you identify opportunities for your knowledge and talents.

My team and I continuously conduct market research for my business. We complete interviews, send questionnaires, and put polls inside our Facebook group. To incentivize responses, we sometimes do a random drawing that gives participants an opportunity to win prizes. The results from our research allow us to stay connected with our target audience and identify ways to improve our offerings and create new products.

There are many ways to evaluate the market. Here are some of my favorites.

Interviews

Start with the list of target markets that might be interested in your product or service. Brainstorm the categories of people you think might be interested in your offering. Then ask your friends, family, and even strangers in online forums if they know someone who fits that persona. Next, schedule time to interview people so you can ask them open-ended questions.

Focus Groups

Get a small group of people together in person or via video conference and have them discuss topics and answer questions relevant to your business idea. This also works particularly well if you have a sample of a product that you want people to test and discuss. I try to keep my focus groups to five people or less.

That way, everyone has a chance to talk. It should be noted that with focus groups, you run the risk of people's initial thoughts on a topic being influenced by the group.

Polls and Surveys

Surveys typically require the least amount of time to set up, and depending on how you ask questions, they could require the least amount of time from your target audience. If you offer multiple choice questions, you'll be able to look at the percentage of people who answered each question a certain way. On the flip side, when you do surveys, you lose the opportunity to ask follow-up questions unless you conduct an interview with that person after they complete the survey.

Existing Research

Thanks to the internet, it is possible that someone has already conducted research on your industry and target market. I'm a big fan of using Google Trends and Google Scholar to find information that already exists. You can do this type of research without even leaving your house or speaking to another person. That being said, if you want your specific questions answered and to have control on the data size, conducting your own research is a great way to go.

Research is something I still do regularly in my business. It helps me stay connected to changes within the industry and continue to deliver to my target audience what they want. While every research method has its pros and cons, I'm personally a big fan of using a combination of methods to get to know a target market. In writing this book, I used polls, interviews, and focus groups to make sure the content I covered would be of interest and value.

YOU'RE NOT LOOKING FOR EVERYONE!

While I lived in Boston, I often attended events that helped people build and develop their start-up or small business. At one event, I had the opportunity to sign up for a mentoring session with someone who invested in start-ups.

We were discussing why start-ups fail, and he shared how founders often try to be everything to everyone. He then said the following:

> Picture yourself at war and that your enemy occupies a beach that you need in order to win. You don't send all of your troops to spread out along the entire beach. You pick the edge of the beach, then you conquer it. Then you conquer the next adjacent section of the beach and so on until you occupy the entire beach. That's what people need to do when they're marketing their business.

While I can't remember the investor's name, he painted a vivid picture in my mind that I have yet to forget. So often I have clients tell me that their product is for everyone. That may be true. But if you try to reach everyone at once, you'll metaphorically spread your troops across the entire beach and lose the war.

Even Apple didn't reach every market at first. In fact, I distinctly remember a time when I was the only person in my family with a Mac and my parents made fun of me. Today, if I visit my parents' house, you can't walk two steps without spotting an Apple product. You can find at least one of the following in almost every room: Apple TV, Apple Watch, MacBook, iPhone, iPad, and Apple charger.

Focusing on a specific target market is important, but it doesn't mean you have to build a business that only serves one audience forever.

While your business may expand to reach many audiences, if you want to see success, you must first validate your idea with one community.

It's in focusing on a small market that you end up touching the world.

Counterintuitive, I know!

Before you can ever scale, you must first succeed with what author and entrepreneur Seth Godin calls your *minimum viable audience.*

FINDING YOUR MINIMUM VIABLE AUDIENCE

In July 2017, Godin published the concept of having a minimum viable audience on his blog. Here's a short excerpt:

> When you seek to engage with everyone, you rarely delight anyone. And if you're not the irreplaceable, essential, one-of-a-kind changemaker, you never get a chance to engage with the market.
>
> The solution is simple but counterintuitive: Stake out the smallest market you can imagine. The smallest market that can sustain you, the smallest market you can adequately serve. This goes against everything you learned in capitalism school, but in fact, it's the simplest way to matter.[12]

Trying to reach "everyone" can dilute your message to the point that you connect with no one.

I learned this from personal experience. I belonged to an organization called Business Network International (BNI) for one year early in my entrepreneurship journey. The biggest takeaway I got from that experience was that you need to have a clear target market in mind.

The BNI meetings took place every week. Every week I'd get 30 seconds to tell the same group of people who I was, what I did, who I served, and what I needed. The idea behind

BNI was to build relationships with people and be each other's source of referrals.

When I started at BNI, I tried to keep it broad. My message sounded like "I'm a marketing person that can help pretty much anyone with marketing-related things."

While my intent was to increase my chances of new business, the result was a room full of people whom I had spoken to week over week for months that had no clue what I did.

Part of entrepreneurship is identifying when something isn't working and trying something new.

I decided to try a new strategy. I got incredibly specific with what I did and who I was looking for. At the next meeting I said something like "I'm a marketing strategist that helps service-based business owners create a plan for generating qualified leads through online marketing." The change made a huge difference in my business. Suddenly people were coming up to me saying, "Oh, *that's* what you do." Many came up to me with specific questions about how I could help them.

For your business, your elevator pitch might sound like "Hi, my name is Kristy, and I work with coaches who have a proven method for getting their private clients results by building an online course so they can reach more people without multiplying their workload. If you know a coach who is overloaded with 1:1 work, wants to make more money, and desires to reach more people online, please connect us via email."

You will not be for everyone, and that is a good thing!

This could feel incredibly limiting, but guess what? You probably don't need that many customers to build a sustainable business. Take the time to do the math. How many customers do you need to reach your financial goals? Said another way: what is the smallest section of the beach that you need to conquer to prove your business is viable?

After you have a number of amazing case studies with the customers you've worked with, you'll find people in other markets looking for the same thing. Suddenly you'll hear, "I'm not a coach, but I do have a proven method for helping athletes become more flexible that I use in my physical therapy practice. Could you help me create an online course?"

The key is to start small to grow big.

IMPLEMENTATION CHECKLIST

In this chapter, we discussed identifying your target audience. Remember, you're not looking to market to everyone right away. Before jumping into the next chapter, use this checklist to make sure you're implementing what you've just learned.

- ❑ Brainstorm every group that would want your expertise and why.
- ❑ Conduct market research to understand who wants your expertise and is willing to pay for it.
- ❑ Choose the smallest audience you will market to first.
- ❑ Sign up for the free companion course to access downloadable worksheets and samples of our market research questions. Head to marketyourgeniusbook.com/chapter3 for access.

In the next chapter, we'll discuss creating an offer you can market to your target audience.

CHAPTER 4

THE PATH TO PROFITABILITY

"Forward is not a straight line.
It's much more exciting, complex, difficult,
gnarly, and uncharted than that."

— Jeni Britton Bauer, artisan ice cream maker and entrepreneur of Jeni's Splendid Ice Creams who had the guts to create flavors, such as ricotta toast with red berry geranium jam and genmaicha and marshmallows[13]

I'll never forget the day a company I was working for received a continuous flow of returns.

Boxes just kept coming back from unsatisfied customers.

The product sold well, but most people sent the product back. Then the negative reviews started trickling in.

No amount of marketing can save a product that people don't like.

You can create the perfect product in your mind, but you won't know how great it is until it has been tested by a sample of your dream customers and improved upon based on their feedback.

YOUR MVP IS YOUR MVO

Before you mass market a product or add a bunch of features to your offering, you need to create the simplest version of your idea and beta test it. This product is called your minimum viable offer (MVO). Your most valuable player is your MVO.

Your MVO is the simplest package or offering you can deliver to your first set of customers that provides them with value. It's the package that will help your customers get a desired result with only the critical features.

When you start with your MVO, you can move faster to working with customers and getting their real-time insight into the features they love and want next.

The key is to focus on the absolute must-haves for your product.

When I first started offering my services, I remember looking at the websites of coaches, consultants, and other entrepreneurs monetizing their knowledge online. The offerings that stood out to me were the ones with bonuses. If a customer bought the product by a deadline, they would receive a bonus of online courses, worksheets, sessions with guest experts, or in-person workshops.

I kept doing the math over and over in my head.

How could I offer all of this and make a profit if I didn't feel ready to charge what my competition was charging?

I was stressing myself out trying to create the perfect program that had everything a customer could ever want.

Then I remembered something my grandmother always said to me as a kid.

K.I.S.S.

In our house, it stood for Keep It Simple, Stupid. And in my company, it stands for Keep It Simple, Sista.

I was overcomplicating things.

I knew from conducting interviews and sending out surveys that my target audience wanted the most help with generating leads and signing clients. They felt like all their marketing efforts generated very little revenue in return.

I took out a piece of paper and wrote down everything I knew they would need to generate leads and get dream customers.

I outlined the information they would need and noted the different types of support I could provide that would help them reach their goals.

Then I crossed off everything that wasn't absolutely necessary to help them get results.

To my surprise, the program was simple, and I was confident it could help others get more dream customers.

The day after I outlined my minimum viable offer, an acquaintance called out of the blue to catch up. During our call, she mentioned that she was launching a new business but wasn't sure where to start. I mentioned that I had just started a business helping entrepreneurs generate leads and get more customers. Before I knew it, she was asking questions about my services.

I read straight off the paper that outlined my MVO. She asked about pricing and I quoted her $3,000 with bonus sessions if paid in full. Within 24 hours she had paid in full.

Less than two days later, I had another client sign on to work with me.

By the time I was ready to market my offering online, I had testimonials and case studies from people who had already worked with me. Plus, I knew how I wanted to adjust the program based on their feedback.

When you create your minimum viable offer, it's important to enroll people into your program quickly. The sooner you start working with customers, the sooner you can get out of your head creating the perfect program and into the field of helping people.

When you're offering a service or a digital product, it should take weeks (not years) to map out your MVO and enroll your first set of customers.

It's not about solving all of your dream customer's problems or attracting everyone who could possibly be interested in your offering. It's about solving an important problem for a small set of customers and gaining momentum in your business. You can do this in five simple steps.

Step 1: Visualize Success

Before I create any product, I write out dream testimonials. I take out a notebook and write what I want people to say about the book, event, or program, as if they've already finished it.

Writing dream testimonials allows me to get crystal clear on the experience I want to deliver to my customers. If you're into manifesting, it also has the added benefit of sharing what you want to happen with the Universe.

To stay connected with your dream testimonials, I also recommend recording what you write down and listening to the recording on a regular basis. The following exercise walks you through how to create your dream testimonials.

The Dream Testimonial Exercise

Picture 10 of your dream customers. They've just completed your offer. Take time and answer the questions below for each of them:

1. What does their testimonial say?
2. What results did they accomplish?
3. How do they feel about working with you and your team?
4. What was their favorite part of the program?
5. What are they saying to their friends about your program?

When you're done, record yourself reading your 10 dream testimonials. Then listen to it at least once a week to connect with the impact you desire your program to make.

Step 2: Choose What to Sell

For a long time, I thought that if I left corporate my only option was to become a consultant. I thought this meant spending my days meeting with local clients and helping them build and implement their marketing strategies.

After hiring my first private coach, I discovered there were multiple ways to monetize one's genius.

To give you an idea, here are a list of 12 ways people monetize their genius:

1. Consulting or done-for-you services
2. Coaching services
3. Online courses
4. Software
5. Books
6. Stationery and office goods (journals, planners, notebooks, etc.)
7. Branded merchandise (T-shirts, mugs, etc.)
8. Membership sites
9. Seminars, retreats, workshops, and other events
10. Speakerships
11. Sponsorships (selling ad space on podcasts, blogs, vlog, etc.)
12. Affiliates

These 12 monetization methods may seem like a lot, but they can be grouped into five categories:

Merch and physical products

Online and digital products

Networking opportunities, events, and experiences

Endorsements

Your time

Or M.O.N.E.Y for short.

You get to choose the method that is most aligned to your customer needs, audience size, revenue goals, talents, and lifestyle preferences. As you think about your minimum viable product, ask yourself which delivery method is right for you and your customers.

For more support choosing your monetization method, head to marketyourgeniusbook.com/chapter4 for videos and worksheets.

Step 3: Land Your First Customers

You first customers will likely come from one of the following sources:

- People you connected with during your market research
- People you know personally who have the problem your MVO solves
- People who are connected to your friends, family, and acquaintances

You will never have 100 percent control over where your leads come from, but you will always have 100 percent control over your actions to attract them.

Without a crystal ball and magical powers, you cannot determine the exact time a specific person will buy your MVO. That being said, you can take actions that will help you initially sell your minimum viable product. Here are some of my favorites.

Reconnect with Your Market Research Pool

At the end of a survey, interview, or focus group, ask if the person is interested in hearing more about the product or service you are doing research on. There will be people who say no. There will also be people who say yes.

Make note of the people who stated that they would like to hear about your offering. Invite them to a call to discover if your offering is the solution to their problem.

Ask Your Network for Referrals

You may want to keep friendship and business separate, but that doesn't mean your friends can't support you.

One of my first clients came from a friend that I didn't even ask to refer me. My friend had a crystal-clear picture of what I did and how I could help someone. When she ran into someone with the very problem I helped solve, she sent them my way.

When you ask your network for referrals, it's important to give them a clear picture of who you're looking to work with and how you can help them.

For example, if you're a career counselor, you may only get referrals when someone is looking to switch jobs or careers. But if you ask your network to listen for people who say they don't love their job but they're not sure what to do next, you may get more referrals.

Go through your phone, Facebook, LinkedIn, and Instagram accounts. Create a list of 100 people in your network that you're committed to connecting or reconnecting with. Then reach out to five different people on your list every day.

Remember, you have no way of knowing exactly who will know someone who could be an ideal client. But by catching up with people, getting a sense of what they're up to, and sharing what you've been doing, you're bound to find someone who has a referral for you; plus you'll reconnect with people you haven't spoken to in a while.

Think Rich and Have Faith

A few weeks before I signed my first two clients, I started to read the book *Think and Grow Rich* by Napoleon Hill. Within the first few chapters of the book, Hill outlines six steps to acquire wealth. The steps are summarized below:

> **Step 1:** Think about the specific amount of money you desire. Know exactly how much you want to make.
>
> **Step 2:** Identify what you'll do in exchange for the money. Will you work with private clients? Sell cake? Teach workshops?
>
> **Step 3:** Determine by when you'd like to have the money. Choose a specific date.
>
> **Step 4:** Create a game plan for bringing in the money and get into action immediately.
>
> **Step 5:** Write a statement that paraphrases everything you outlined in steps 1 to 4.
>
> **Step 6:** Read your statement twice a day, ideally when you wake up in the morning and before you go to bed.[14]

I wrote out my statement and read it every morning and every night.

I choose to believe that this made a huge difference in attracting my first few clients from week one of starting my business. It's one of the reasons I continue to follow these steps today.

You could have the perfect game plan for landing your first few customers, but you need to believe that it's possible. When you believe you will bring on new customers, you can continue to take action even when it doesn't look as though anything is happening. Reading a statement every day helped me believe that my goal was possible.

Step 4: Build In Feedback Loops

One of my former bosses used to say, "Feedback is a gift."

When you're launching your business, feedback is one of the best gifts you can receive.

If you're selling a service, I recommend scheduling check-in sessions at the midway point and at the end of your offering if you are doing a multiple-month package.

The intention of these calls (or surveys) is to ensure that your customers are getting the most out of their experience working with you and to identify areas of improvement.

At the midpoint session, the goal is to get a sense of how your client is liking the program (and why), what they're not liking (and why), and what results they are currently seeing. And by checking in at least once before the end of the program, you're able to pinpoint what's working and what's not working with the program you've designed.

Ideally, before the end of the program, you will have identified what could make it better and will have started making those adjustments. Even if you aren't selling a service, you want your first set of customers to tell you what they think about your offering and share how your offering is helping them get results. This information is priceless.

Until you start servicing customers, you have no idea what results people will get from your offering.

Here's what one of my early clients had to say about their experience.

> I came to her having zero business knowledge, and she helped me get up to speed, learn how to treat my business like a business (instead of a hobby), and most importantly, helped me have major breakthroughs around what was really calling me in my business. Funny enough, I came to her wanting to start a videography business, but during our time together, she helped me come to the realization that video was not what I was truly after in my career. The advice and support she gave me was priceless.

This particular client was not the only person I worked with who was building the business they thought they were qualified for instead of what they were passionate about.

It's because of these early clients that I started helping entrepreneurs identify the business they can see themselves happily running 5, 10, and 15 years into the future before the first session. This was not initially built into the program.

Implementation leads to vital information.

Step 5: Decide on Your Price

There's a difference between offering a free haircut or some free coaching to improve your skills and creating a minimum viable offer. It should not exist to test your skills at something new. Remember, it's the simplest package or offering you can deliver to your first set of customers that provides them with value and helps them achieve a result.

Your minimum viable offer exists to help you launch quickly, start helping people get results, and identify the holes in your process or offering so you can quickly fill them. It ensures that you are not mass marketing a product or service that people do not like. Remember the daily shipment of returns?

Instead of offering your MVO for free, I recommend that you come up with an initial beta offer that takes into consideration the value of your offering and the cost to deliver it.

THE VALUE

I believe in pricing an offering in such a way that the value is at least 5 to 10 times what your client is paying. Said another way, if a program costs $100, ideally the value would be between $500 to $1,000.

This chart gives suggested pricing based on the perceived value of your offering. If you believe that for your market, the distance between the price and the perceived value should be greater, lower your price accordingly.

	VALUE RANGE	
Price	**5 x**	**10 x**
$100	**$500**	**$1,000**
$1,000	**$5,000**	**$10,000**
$3,000	**$15,000**	**$30,000**
$5,000	**$25,000**	**$50,000**
$10,000	**$50,000**	**$100,000**

This value could be money saved, money earned, or outcomes your clients perceive as valuable.

Let's say you're in the business of helping people lose and keep off weight. Between self-help books, apps, special food, and gym memberships, let's say your ideal customer spends

$5,000 per year trying to lose weight. You have a proven track record of helping people lose weight and keep it off for at least 10 years without a gym membership or special foods and supplements. If your program is $5,000, then by enrolling in your program, your prospective clients could save $45,000 over a 10-year period by working with you instead of continuing on their own.

	10-YEAR PERIOD	STATUS
PROSPECTIVE CLIENT	**$50,000 ($5,000/year X 10 years)**	**Still trying to achieve goal**
CURRENT CLIENT	**$5,000**	**Reached and maintained goal**
SAVINGS	**$45,000**	

The $45,000 savings (aka perceived value) falls within the $25,000 to $50,000 suggested value range for a $5,000 offering.

But let's pretend this weight-loss expert couldn't quantify the money saved.

What would it be worth for a parent to be more active with their children, prevent health problems, or extend their life? Sometimes the value cannot be quantified numerically, and that's okay. The question remains: will it be worth the investment?

THE COST TO DELIVER

While your product or service should be of high value to your clients or customers, it should cost you less to deliver it. According to the Corporate Finance Institute, while it varies by industry, in general a 20 percent profit margin is considered good while a 5 percent profit margin is considered low.[15]

Your goal is to have the highest profit margin possible while creating and maintaining the best experience and product possible.

While your profit margins will fluctuate based on the products you produce and the stage of growth your business is in, if you're launching a MVO with only your talents and your computer, you should be able to maintain a low cost and a high profit margin.

Even if you think you're barely spending money to run your business, take the time to get intimate with your numbers.

In Chapter 1, I shared how I generated six figures in revenue while getting myself into tremendous debt. Had I created a profit and loss statement (P&L) and looked at the money that was going out in addition to what was coming in, I would have been more profitable in my early years.

Pricing is an art and a science. When you're launching your first product, remember that your pricing isn't permanent. That being said, you should determine if you are a low-cost brand, premium brand, or somewhere in between. While you can change your pricing, if you start off by charging $100 for a product, it will be hard for you to increase the price to $100,000 unless there is a big shift in market demand or perceived value. But if your first few clients are offered a $10,000 product for $7,500 and it will never be that price again, you're at least in the same ballpark and offering your first customers an incentive for working with you early.

It is critical to validate your proof of concept and product-to-market fit with a minimum viable offer before allocating large amounts of money or resources to marketing your business. With that in mind, you want to make it easy for people to say yes to your minimum viable offer without making it so far off from your future goal price. It's an art and a science.

IMPLEMENTATION CHECKLIST

Before jumping into the next chapter, here's a list of action items to make sure you implement what you've learned so far so you know you have an offering people want.

- ❑ Make a list of everything your dream customer needs to know or have to get the result you will help them achieve. Then cross out everything that isn't crucial to their success.
- ❑ Reconnect with your friends, family, acquaintances, and market research pool. Remember, it's about building relationships, not forcing sales.
- ❑ Write out your Think & Grow Rich statement and read it daily.
- ❑ Sign up for the free companion course to access downloadable worksheets and training videos. Head to marketyourgeniusbook.com/chapter4 for access.

In the next chapter, we'll start mapping out a marketing and sales plan for generating consistent customers.

PART II

HOW TO PROMOTE YOUR GENIUS

In the "promote" stage, you are getting your offer on your target audience's radar, filling your pipeline with qualified leads, and generating a consistent flow of customers. The goal of this phase is to create and validate a plan to reach your target audience, help them identify if your offer is right for them, and invite them to buy.

Chapter 5: Just Like Dating. To have a consistent flow of customers, you must first generate a consistent flow of leads. In this chapter, you'll:

- Select your strategy for getting in front of your target audience.
- Decide how you will capture your target audience's attention so you get on their radar.
- Determine the value you will give your target audience in exchange for their contact information.

Chapter 6: Give It Away Now. Once you have new leads, it is time to give them the information they need to choose to buy from you or not. In this chapter, you'll:

- Learn the difference between cold, warm, and hot leads so you can provide prospects with the right information at the right time.
- Discover how content marketing can help you educate your leads and build trust so they are more likely to buy from you.
- Build a game plan for turning cold leads into warm leads and warm leads into hot leads.

Chapter 7: Signed, Sealed, Delivered. With a pipeline filled with hot leads, it's time to convert them into customers. In this chapter, you'll:

- Plan your pre-sales activities so your hot leads can easily buy your products and services.
- Build your sales system so you can consistently turn hot leads into customers with ease.
- Learn how to approach sales so you are confident and present during sales conversations.

Chapter 8: Test Like a M.A.A.D. Scientist. Once you have a sales and marketing plan drafted, it's time to make sure it will consistently work for your business. In this chapter, you'll:

- Discover how to validate your sales and marketing plans.
- Learn the M.A.A.D. Scientist framework so your plan consistently gets results.
- Identify the metrics you'll need to track so you know if your strategy is going according to plan.

CHAPTER 5

JUST LIKE DATING

"If anything at all, perfection is not when there is nothing to add, but when there is nothing left to take away."[16]

— Maria Tallchief, the first American prima ballerina who refused to change her last name despite guidance to do so. She spoke out against injustices and discrimination, never forgetting her Native American heritage.[17]

When I worked at the tech start-up, my side hustle was teaching digital marketing classes for General Assembly, an education and career transformation company. As a lead marketing instructor, I taught everything from three-hour workshops to 10-week courses. During class, people often asked me how to create the perfect marketing plan, the plan that would work for their unique business and consistently generate leads and create customers.

My answer was always the same. A great marketing plan is one that is simple to track and execute. I'd then share that marketing is just like dating. Then I would tell a story about dating to illustrate the components of a strong marketing plan.

In my early 20s, my friends and I would go to bars to find prospective partners. The hunt for an eligible bachelor began with choosing where we were going to spend the evening. We had to choose somewhere that we believed our dream guy would hang out.

After getting all done up, we'd go out to the bar. This is where things got interesting. Believe it or not, I would get incredibly nervous and shy when we went out. When I saw someone I thought was cute, the idea of making eye contact or inviting them over made me want to run for the hills. Luckily, I had a best friend who had my back. Maria would either invite a guy over or convince me to sit by myself and smile at the guy. The idea was to capture his attention and spark a conversation. Some other tactics I tried were "accidentally" bumping into someone or paying them a compliment.

Once I had someone's attention, we'd start talking. For most of the conversation, I had the thought, *Please ask me for my number*, running through my mind. If the conversation went well and we seemed to like each other enough to keep talking, there was an exchange of numbers or sometimes even a date scheduled right on the spot.

For me, the entire goal of exchanging numbers was to get a date. During the first date, my hope was for things to go well enough for there to be a second date. And then a third date. And so on, until you were officially and exclusively dating. After dating for a while, the idea was to make the decision, as my grandmother would say, to "piss or get off the pot." Said another way, we were either heading for a lifetime together or calling it quits.

Marketing is just like dating. In fact, my strategy for dating has the same steps you need to take to consistently generate leads for your business, build a relationship with those leads, and turn them into dream customers.

In this chapter, we'll map out your game plan for attracting leads for your business so you can start filling your pipeline with potential customers.

FINDING YOUR AUDIENCE

If you feel as though you're spending your days hoping that your marketing activities will bring you your next dream client, you're not alone. The key to consistently creating dream customers is to first understand where your dream customers are spending their time on and offline.

Large companies have the team, money, and resources to be on every social media platform 24/7. Trying to do what they do is like you racing someone on the Olympic track and field team.

You don't need to be everywhere, you just need to be in the right places to find and attract your audience. The best way to find your target audience is by asking people who meet your dream client qualifications where they spend their time on and offline.

What social media platforms are they on most frequently?

What conferences do they regularly attend?

What networking organizations or associations do they belong to?

What websites do they love?

Whose email list are they on?

What are they googling or researching online?

The goal is to get into their head so you can determine where you can consistently show up and meet dream customers.

You Down with O.P.P.?

Most people get in front of their audience using at least one of the following methods.

Organic. From a digital marketing perspective, organic marketing is the act of creating and sharing content optimized for discovery. Said another way, it means putting out a prolific amount of content in such a way that your target audience finds it. They could find it through a search engine, hashtags, their newsfeed, etc.

You can also share your content with journalists who are looking for tips or quotes for their latest assignment.

If you're building your business through offline marketing tactics, this could mean going to networking events and organically meeting people.

The key to organic marketing activities is to do them consistently. It often takes time to determine what works best and to start yielding results.

Paid. Paid marketing allows you to get in front of your target audience much more quickly. It typically consists of running ads to your targeted audience. You can run ads on specific social media platforms, on websites your target market reads, or in newspapers, magazines, or trade publications. You can also sponsor conferences and events where you know your target audience will spend their time.

The key to mastering paid marketing activities is to do smaller-size tests to identify what works best before spending a large amount of money. When you choose your budget, expect to spend some money to figure out what's working and what isn't.

Partnerships. If you love connecting with people or have a network of people who have a following you want to get in front of, building strategic partnerships is another great way to connect with potential customers. With strategic partnerships, someone else's audience is being introduced to you. This can be done by shoutouts on social media, driving traffic to your site or products via an email newsletter, or inviting you to speak to their audience.

The key to mastering partnerships is to remember that it's about building relationships. It's a give-and-take strategy where you need to be sure you're also delivering value to your strategic partners so the relationship continues to be mutually beneficial.

CAPTURING ATTENTION

Getting in front of your target audience is only part of the equation. You have to capture their attention if you want a chance at a "first date."

If you're marketing your business online, this means creating content that is so compelling your target audience will stop what they're doing to engage with your content.

Think about the last time you stopped scrolling through your newsfeed to read something or the last time you picked up a magazine, newspaper, or book. What made you stop what you were doing to engage?

For most people, it's a strong headline and a compelling first few sentences or few seconds of content.

To create something that captures the attention of your target audience, you have to know them better than their best friend. When you're able to get inside of their head and share content they want to read, watch, or listen to, you've done your job.

Someone who I think is great at this is Derrick Jaxn, self-love ambassador, entrepreneur, and author of *Don't Forget Your Crown*. Derrick creates short videos with headlines like "How to Stop Being Taken for Granted," "4 Signs You May Be a Fixer," "Why He Expects You to Chase Him," and "How to Know for Sure He's a Real One."

He is very clear on his target audience of single women and creates content they want to consume.

Whether you are capturing the attention of your target audience online or offline, your job is to get inside their head and identify the words, topics, and thoughts they are having on a regular basis.

GETTING THE DIGITS

Once you have your audience's attention, the key is to metaphorically get their "digits." If you're in person, this could mean getting their business card. Online, this could mean getting their email in exchange for a valuable piece of content.

In dating, someone usually gives you their contact information because they are interested in speaking to you further and seeing where things go.

In business, however, there is typically more resistance to giving out contact information. No one wants to be spammed with messages or overly sold to. Your job is to make it feel worthwhile for your target audience to give you their contact information. That means having a compelling reason for your audience to opt in to hearing from you.

A company that's masterful at this is HubSpot. HubSpot is a software company that helps their customers manage and automate sales and marketing activities. When you go to their blog, they have hundreds, if not thousands, of articles designed to help you solve a business problem. With each article, there's an offer to get a template, cheat sheet, or guide that will provide even more support on the topic you're reading about.

For example, if you read an article about email marketing, you will likely see an offer to download an "Email Marketing

Planning Template." To download the template, all you need to do is provide them with your email address. In the marketing world, we call this a lead magnet, freebie, or content upgrade. It's something compelling that you offer a prospective lead in exchange for their contact information. You can put your lead magnet on your website or include the URL to it on your business cards.

THE ANATOMY OF A GREAT LEAD MAGNET

The key to having a great lead magnet is to create something that has the following qualities:

It isn't a big commitment. Your first date usually isn't a seven-day vacation with a stranger. It's often coffee or drinks at a bar. The idea is that you don't want to make the commitment too large in case you realize you don't really like one another. Think of your main lead magnet in the same way. What you offer your audience should be something that doesn't take them hours to get through or use.

Your target audience wants it. If your date doesn't drink alcohol, you might not want to take them to the bar for your first date. The same holds true for your lead magnet. Think of something your target audience would find useful or valuable. I can't stress enough the importance of getting to know your target audience well. Using HubSpot as an example, if you know your target audience is interested in email marketing, then offering an "Email Marketing Planning Template" is a great way to quickly give them value.

**A great lead magnet is like a great first date.
It leaves your prospect excited for the next one.**

It clearly relates to what you do. Part of dating is getting to know one another and seeing if you're a match. That's why it's so important to allow people to get to know the real you, not just who you think they want. When you're creating your lead magnet, you want to do the same thing. Make sure it showcases who you are as a brand and that it relates to what you do, not just what your target market would find valuable. For example, I may know that my target market is looking for love and a lead magnet they may want are tips for online dating. But that has nothing to do with what I can help them with. I help people build profitable businesses from their stories and skills. Therefore, my lead magnet should be closely related to building a profitable "experts" business.

BUILDING YOUR LEAD GENERATION SYSTEM

If you want a consistent flow of leads, you need to build a system or process for it. Now that you have an idea of the high-level process for generating leads, it's time to build a system specifically for you. Here are the steps for building your lead generation system.

Step 1: Choose Where You Are Going to Connect with Your Target Audience

You don't need to be everywhere in order to generate leads for your business. In fact, I recommend that you choose one place to start with until you have a clear and repeatable system for generating leads.

Note that I recommend you start with one method so you can focus on understanding the messages and activities that work for your business. Once you have it down, I recommend that you find at least two other sources for leads.

At the beginning of the COVID-19 pandemic, I had a number of clients whose main source of leads was through in-person speaking gigs. All of their scheduled speaking engagements were either canceled or postponed indefinitely. This is why it's so important to have more than one source of leads. You never know what can happen. The sooner you create and test a system for one lead source, the sooner you can create and test at least two more so a major event doesn't halt your progress.

Step 2: Identify How You Will Capture Their Attention

Once you know where you're going to meet your target audience, you want to get clear on how you're going to capture their attention. Will you post content online that they can't wait to engage with? Will you wear an interesting shirt at a networking event?

The main goal is to capture the attention of your target audience and spark a conversation with a potential lead. Don't be afraid to get creative. Just remember to stay true to your brand.

Here are a few ways you can capture your audience's attention.

- Share three to seven tips for getting a result. Take a tip out of BuzzFeed's playbook and come up with an odd-numbered list of tips or tricks that your target audience will want to read.
- Write an interesting or shocking headline for a 90-second video to stop your target audience from scrolling so they can get value from your content. For inspiration, pay attention to what stops you from scrolling when reading a news site or looking at a social media feed.

- Wear a T-shirt or carry a bag that has a saying that resonates with your target audience. At a conference I was speaking at, I wore a shirt that said, "Do More of What Makes You Happy." Many people stopped me to comment on my shirt, and it was a natural conversation starter for why I left my corporate job to start my business.

Step 3: Create a Lead Magnet to Offer in Exchange for Contact Information

Use a tool such as Canva, Microsoft Word, Adobe InDesign, or Google Sheets to create a lead magnet. The goal is to provide something *valuable*. If you're not tech-savvy or gifted in design, you can also choose to work with a graphic designer, hire someone on Fiverr, or buy a template from Creative Market or Etsy to create your lead magnet. Think of your lead magnet as a first impression. It shouldn't be the feature film, rather it should be the trailer.

Here are some lead magnet ideas:

- Short assessment
- Quiz
- Checklist
- Template
- Road map to getting a result
- List of steps to accomplish a goal
- Discount on the first purchase of your products (particularly physical products)

Head to marketyourgeniusbook.com/chapter5 for a full list of lead magnet ideas.

Step 4: Decide What Contact Information You Want and How You Will Get It

Depending on your business, you may prefer to have one or more ways to connect with your leads. Just remember, the more you ask for, the less likely it is for someone to give you any information.

Imagine if before the first date, someone asked you for your birthday, phone number, email address, home address, and Instagram handle. You might take it as a sign to run far away. Treat your lead generation system the same way. Keep it simple and make it easy to sign up for your lead magnet.

There are tools like HubSpot and Leadpages that allow you to create a page for someone to enter their email address then automatically get your lead magnet so you don't have to manually send it to everyone who asks for it. They even have features that allow someone to text a number to get your lead magnet.

When you put all of these steps together, you have a repeatable process for generating leads.

To get new leads, you don't need 1,000 different tactics. You just need one tactic that brings 1,000 leads over and over again.

Here are some sample lead generation systems.

Sample #1

1. Get introduced to your target audience by being a guest on a podcast.
2. Tell stories about how you and your clients have gone from where your target audience currently is to where they desperately want to be. Then give them a few tips on how to make it possible.

3. Let the audience know that they can get a free template that will make their life easier.
4. Share that all they need to do is text a number and send you their email address to get the free template.

Sample #2

1. Share links to a blog post every day on LinkedIn using specific hashtags.
2. Use headlines in your post that will capture the attention of your target audience.
3. Let the audience know that they can get a free template that will make their life easier.
4. Share that all they need to do is join your Facebook group to get the free template.

Sample #3

1. Go to events you know your target audience will be at.
2. Spark conversations with people at the event.
3. When you meet someone who is a good potential fit for your products or services, tell them about your "freebie" and ask if they want it.
4. Get their email address and permission to sign them up for your freebie, letting them know that they'll also be on your email list and can unsubscribe at anytime.

MAPPING OUT YOUR LEAD GENERATION SYSTEM

Now it's your turn. Take a few moments to answer the following questions for your business.

- What one place will you focus on to connect with your target audience?
- How will you capture their attention?
- What will you offer in exchange for their contact information?
- How can they quickly and easily get that offer? And what information do they need to give you to receive the free offer?

When you have your answers, start building your lead generation system and put it into action.

IMPLEMENTATION CHECKLIST

Before jumping into the next chapter, use the below checklist to make sure you have implemented what you've just learned.

- ❑ Make a list of where your target audience spends their time on- or offline.
- ❑ Brainstorm the topics, phrases, or headlines that would capture your target audience's attention.
- ❑ Outline your lead generation system.
- ❑ Sign up for the free companion course to see examples of our lead magnets. Head to marketyourgeniusbook.com/chapter5 for access.

In the next chapter, we'll discuss how you can build a relationship with your leads so they can choose to buy from you (or not).

CHAPTER 6

GIVE IT AWAY NOW

"Being dedicated to someone else or to a group of people will make you your best self."[18]

— Jessica Jackley, co-founder of Kiva, "the world's first crowdfunding site for microenterprises"[19] and a catalyst for change in developing communities

I once accepted a Facebook friend request from a fellow entrepreneur who helped women grow their businesses to six figures and beyond. Soon after, I received a DM (direct message) that said, "Really great to connect! Look forward to learning more about you on here. 😁 Have a great day! P.S. I like your profile pic."

I didn't have a chance to respond immediately, and the next day I received another message that said, "It's so lovely to be connected with you. I love what you do. And I believe you would benefit from what I have to offer. I had a look at your profile. And after seeing that, I feel like you would benefit highly by joining my exclusive [Facebook group] where I share a lot of value around how to grow your business to [six figures and beyond]." The message then continued to invite me to the group and included the link.

Since I had already achieved six figures and beyond, I wrote back and said, "Thanks for the friend request. I'm just getting back onto Facebook—left for a while. Curious what specifically had you reach out and invite me to your group. Mainly asking because I already [hit that business milestone]. Xx"

This person did not respond and unfriended me.

Remember, your prospective customers are people first. Treat them how you want to be treated. #GoldenRule

In dating, this experience would be the equivalent of walking up to a stranger and asking them to go on a date with you without ever having a conversation then abruptly walking away if the person didn't say yes.

I do not know if this Facebook approach worked well for this person or not. What I can say is that in my experience, people like to have at least one conversation before they're metaphorically asked on a first date by a stranger.

In this chapter, we'll map out your game plan for building a relationship with your leads such that you take them from being curious about your content to rating themselves an 8, 9, or 10 in how likely they are to buy your product or service.

IT ALL STARTS WITH TRUST

In the last chapter we discussed your lead generating system, the process by which you meet potential leads, spark a conversation, and collect their contact information.

Once you have someone's contact information, it's the responsibility of your lead nurturing system to take your cold leads and turn them into hot leads.

Your leads are not all at the same part of the buying cycle.

Cold, Warm, and Hot Leads

Have you noticed how you've warmed up to some potential mates faster than others? For the most part, they all start at the same stage: you're interested but still feeling them out. Then at some point you start visualizing yourself dating this person and if the dating experience goes well, you might even consider staying with them long-term.

This same experience is true for your potential clients.

Cold Leads. A cold lead is a potential client or customer who has given you their contact information but has not yet expressed interest in buying your products or services.

Oftentimes these are people who have recently been introduced to your brand. When your target audience "meets" you for the first time, they're usually evaluating you. They may be asking themselves, *Do I like what they have to say? Do I connect with them? Do they have content or information I want?*

The goal with cold leads is to build trust, add value, and create interest for your products or services. One of the simplest ways to do this is to create a sequence of emails that your new lead will receive once they sign up for your freebie. As a quick reminder, your freebie is something compelling that you offer a prospective lead in exchange for their contact information.

Depending on your product, it could take a lot of interactions before a cold lead becomes a warm lead.

Warm Leads. A warm lead is a potential customer who knows you or your brand well. This could be someone who frequently visits your blog or opens up every email you send. They already resonate with your message and look forward to hearing from you.

The goal is to get out of the "friend zone." This type of lead may love your content but has not put your offerings on their to-buy list. For some, it's because they're not ready to make an investment. For others, it's because they haven't found a compelling reason to focus on the area of life you can help them with. For example, I've had clients who needed a year before they were ready to really focus on building their business. Before that, they simply enjoyed reading about it and dreaming about it.

To get out of the friend zone, your job is to show warm leads what's possible when they start investing time, energy, or money into the problem you can help them solve. For example, a person may want to find a relationship but believe they need to focus on their career first. If you have a compelling reason for focusing on finding a partner now instead of waiting for career satisfaction, then you may invite your warm leads to a webinar to help shift their mindset.

Hot Leads. Hot leads are potential customers who have taken actions that indicate they are very interested in your product or service but have not made the purchase. For example, this could be someone who heads to the sales page on your website, requests a demo, completes a "learn more form," or frequently visits your store and browses.

Hot leads may not have all the information they need to make a buying decision or may not have a compelling reason to buy now.

The goal with hot leads is to provide information that will help them make a buying decision now. An easy way to do this is to either conduct a product demo, share customer success stories, or provide a special discount code if they buy now.

MANAGING CUSTOMER RELATIONSHIPS

As your business grows, you will go from managing a handful of leads to managing thousands or even millions of people. This will make it increasingly important for you to have a system that manages and automatically tags leads as cold, warm, or hot.

This is the value of having a customer relationships management (CRM) system that can also do what we marketers call marketing automation.

What the Heck Is a CRM System?

A CRM system is technology that allows you to manage relationships with your potential and actual customers. A great CRM will store contact information, keep notes of your conversations, tag where people are in the buying cycle, and email them directly from your tool.

The role of a CRM is to help you streamline your processes, always know when you last connected with a lead and what you said, and not let leads fall through the cracks.

What the Heck Is Marketing Automation?

Marketing automation is a tool or software that allows you to automate different marketing activities. A simple example goes back to offering a freebie. When someone signs up for your freebie, the software will automatically add their name and contact information to your list and send them a sequence of emails across a certain period of days.

What gets exciting for a marketing nerd like me is when you have a system that can track a lead's different actions, such as visiting your blog, frequenting a sales page, or choosing certain answers on your application. Then the system automatically tags them as a cold, warm, or hot lead and sends them specific information based on that tag. It can even help you know if someone you haven't spoken to would be interested in joining your Facebook group so you don't make the offer prematurely.

It's like having someone track and evaluate the behavior of your potential mates behind the scenes to determine if they're a strong candidate for you or not.

It sounds a bit creepy, but it is incredibly valuable for you and your lead. If someone just heard about you and is not even sure what your products are yet, they probably will not want a bunch of sales messages from you.

There are many systems that will allow you to manage customer relationships and implement marketing automation at varying price points. A list of CRMs can be found inside the free companion course at marketyourgeniusbook.com/chapter6.

Repeat after Me: Keep It Simple, Sista

I've taught enough marketing courses to know that by now, some people may be feeling a bit overwhelmed by what I've shared so far. If that's you, don't skip this mini recap.

The key to building a lead nurturing system is to understand that it's all about building a relationship with your leads in such a way that they are ready to buy from you. You want to avoid metaphorically walking up to a stranger at a bar and saying, "Hey, want to get married?"

To do this, you have to know where your relationship is with each of your leads at any given time. Have you just met?

Then they are a cold lead. Are they expressing interest in your products or content but haven't added anything to their cart? Then they're a warm lead. Or do they frequently go to your sales page or have your product in their shopping cart? Then you have what we've been working toward: a hot lead.

There are tools that will automatically update your relationship status with your leads and send them emails or ads based on their behavior. These are marketing automation tools with customer relationship management (CRM) features.

CONTENT THAT CONNECTS

I often see ads that say how content is dead and that they have a new strategy to help you build your business—all you need to do is watch their webinar.

These ads crack me up because their ad was a piece of content and so is their webinar.

According to the Content Marketing Institute, "Content marketing is a strategic marketing approach focused on creating and distributing valuable, relevant, and consistent content to attract and retain a clearly defined audience—and, ultimately, to drive profitable customer action."[20]

I believe content is anything someone can read, listen to, or watch for information, inspiration, or entertainment. That means your blog posts, webinars, podcast episodes, YouTube videos, live videos, photographs on social media, and so much more are all pieces of content.

Content is one of the best ways to nurture relationships with your leads online. In the offline world, you might meet a lead for coffee, host an event, or have a phone call. In the online world, you can create different pieces of content and share them with leads when they reach a certain status in your relationship.

For cold leads, you may send them specific blog posts or podcast episodes based on their current interests.

For warm leads, you may send them client case studies or product demonstrations.

For hot leads, you may send them an invitation to book a sales call with you and a video detailing the benefits of your product or service.

When done strategically, content can help you introduce yourself to your audience, add value, answer frequently asked questions, spark interest in your products, remove objections to buying your product or service, and drive people to buy now.

To create content effectively, you must have a plan.

A Plan for Consistent Content

The real key to nurturing relationships with leads is being consistent. Being present for a period of time then disappearing will be noticed, no matter the size of your audience. No one wants to be ghosted. To ensure you're consistently creating and sharing content that will help leads determine if they want to buy from you or not, I recommend creating and releasing a consistent flow of content.

Weekly Content

If you only have a little bit of time each week for content, focus on a weekly show. Think of it like your favorite program on television. It comes out at the same time each week like clockwork. You anticipate watching it because it's so good, you can't miss it! You might even plan your schedule around the program.

> **Don't be the friend who only calls when they want something. Be the friend that's there no matter what.**

You can nurture leads by creating the same experience for your business. This could be a live video, YouTube video, podcast, blog post, or email newsletter. The idea is to show up at the same time each week and add value.

A great way to come up with the content for your weekly show is to play the 100 questions game. The 100 questions game is when you write down 100 questions, concerns, or tips that will help an ideal customer make a decision to work with you or not. If you designed a sleep training app, this could be 100 questions your target audience has about sleep training. If you help people lose weight, this could be 100 questions your target audience has about weight loss. The goal is to stretch yourself to come up with 100 questions or subtopics you can use for content. If you get stuck, ask your audience to fill out a survey, comment on a social media post, or reply to your email with their biggest challenge or question. Then, each week on your weekly show, you can tackle one of the items on your list. You'll have more than enough to get you through the year. The goal is to have a long-form weekly show you can later repurpose across social media platforms, in emails, or for a book. Creating a weekly show will help you build a reputation of being an expert on a particular subject.

Daily Content

Once you've created your weekly content, you can turn it into smaller pieces of content you can post throughout the week. For example, my team and I release at least one podcast episode each week. Then we turn these episodes into video clips, quote graphics, images, audiograms, and blog posts. We repurpose enough material to have at least one piece of content to post every day that week then share that content on our social media platforms.

Monthly Content

Each month, we do a live masterclass where we tell our audience what they need to do in order to get their desired results for a specific task or goal, show them that it's possible for them, and invite them to join our membership program. This type of content is called conversion content. Examples of conversion content are five-day challenges, webinars, or three-part video series. Its purpose is to convert leads into customers.

To be effective, you'll want to make a plan for how frequently you will create conversion content and put it on your calendar. While we do this content monthly, you may decide it is better for your business to do it more or less frequently.

A Quick Lesson in the Power of Video

There was a night when I was out with my friends in NYC, not far from where I lived. On my way to the bathroom, I saw someone who I thought I went to school with and started to approach them. About 10 feet before I reached them, I realized they were not an old friend at all. In fact, this person was a reality TV star that I had seen on TV a few times.

This is the power of video. Watching someone on video can trick your brain into believing that you've met them in real life. It is one of the many reasons why I recommend that our clients create video content. It allows you to quickly build trust and give people a sense of your brand in a quick and digestible way. As an added bonus, you can turn videos into audio files and transcripts with ease.

BUILDING YOUR LEAD NURTURING SYSTEM

Your lead nurturing system puts together everything we've discussed so far and turns it into a game plan for identifying interested buyers and providing them with the information they need to make a decision that's right for them. These are the steps for building such a system.

Step 1: Determine How You Will Identify Cold, Warm, and Hot Leads

One message doesn't fit all. Your first job in building your lead nurturing system is to identify what actions or inactions would classify someone as a cold, warm, or hot lead.

For example, you could choose to identify a cold lead as someone who is new to your audience and opens and reads your emails but who has not visited a sales page, booked a sales call, or requested a demo.

You may then identify a warm lead as someone who opens and reads all of your emails. Finally, you may identify a hot lead as someone who visited your sales page, completed an application, and checked off in the application that solving their problem was urgent and they're actively seeking support.

Step 2: Determine What Content Your Cold, Warm, and Hot Leads Need to Move Closer to Buying from You

Once you know how you're going to identify each type of lead, it's time to decide what type of content you are going to send.

For cold leads, you may decide to send different emails based on the blog post categories they click on.

For warm leads, you may decide to send specific content based on which sales page they visited or the number of times they visited a sales page.

For hot leads, you may decide which collections of testimonials and case studies you'll send them based on the type of business they have or their business goals.

The key is to determine the types of customers you have and create options that would be best suited for their needs.

Step 3: Make and Implement a Plan to Create Content Consistently

Ask yourself, *What does my lead need to know, believe, or understand in order to effectively make a decision to work with me or not?* When you ask this question for cold, warm, and hot leads, you'll have a better idea of the content you'll need to create. This exercise will also help you come up with items for your "100 questions" list.

Once you have a list of potential content topics, choose the date and time of your weekly show, how much daily content you need to create for each week, and how frequently you will create conversion content.

Step 4: Use Software to Automatically Mark Your Leads as Cold, Warm, or Hot and Send the Relevant Content

After mapping out the ways you'll identify each lead and the content you'll send them, it's time to choose and set up your marketing automation system.

Your marketing automation system will be able to tag or segment your leads based on the behavior you mapped out in Step 1 then send them customized information based on the content you mapped out and created in Steps 2 and 3.

Creating a plan first will make it easier for you to set up or hire someone to set up your marketing automation system effectively.

Completing these four steps are the ultimate goal. But when you're first starting out, the most important step to focus on is number three. Consistently creating and producing content is one of the fastest ways to be perceived as an expert. And conversion content, such as webinars and masterclass series, can help warm up leads and give them a reason to buy now.

SYSTEM EXAMPLES

Now that you have a process for identifying and nurturing leads, let's look at examples of systems for cold, warm, and hot leads.

Cold Lead Example

1. A new person joins your email list after signing up for your free checklist.
2. Your CRM system automatically sends them the checklist, tags them as a cold lead, and puts them in a workflow where they receive a sequence of value-driven emails over a 5- to 10-day period.

Warm Lead Example

1. Someone on your email list opens three emails in a row.
2. They click on the link inside each email that sends them to a blog post.
3. They visit your website three times in a two-day period.

4. Your CRM system tags them as a warm lead and automatically sends them an email inviting them to your free webinar.

Hot Lead Example

1. A person on your list signs up for your webinar.
2. They show up to the webinar and stay to the end.
3. After the webinar, they visit your sales page more than once.
4. Your CRM system tags them as a hot lead and automatically sends them an email with a limited-time offer.

PLANNING YOUR LEAD NURTURING SYSTEM

Now it's your turn. Take a few moments to answer the following questions for your business.

What actions (or inactions) would indicate that your lead is cold?

What actions (or inactions) would indicate that your lead is warm?

What actions (or inactions) would indicate that your lead is hot?

Create your 100 list. What information or beliefs does your target audience need in order to decide to buy from you or not?

What type of content will you create to warm up your leads (live video, pre-recorded video, audio, written)?

Where will you host your weekly content?

How will you turn it into microcontent?

What will your conversion content be and how frequently will you produce it?

IMPLEMENTATION CHECKLIST

Before moving on, make sure to do these action steps from this chapter:

- ❑ Create your dream client non-negotiables list so you can qualify your leads.
- ❑ Come up with 100 questions your target audience wants to know the answers to and use them to plan out your content.
- ❑ Map out your cold, warm, and hot leads nurturing systems.
- ❑ Sign up for the free companion course to access downloadable worksheets and training videos. Head to marketyourgeniusbook.com/chapter6 for access.

When you have hot leads, your next step is to make an offer. In the next chapter, we'll discuss the sales process and how to turn hot leads into customers.

CHAPTER 7

SIGNED, SEALED, DELIVERED

"You can start late, look different, be uncertain, and still succeed."

— Misty Copeland, the first black female ballet dancer to be promoted to principal dancer in the American Ballet Theatre's history. Oh yeah, and she didn't begin to study ballet until the age of 13.[21]

About three months after launching my business, I did my first webinar. I mapped out and delivered a 45-minute training on how to price and package your offerings then differentiate your offering from your competitors.

I emailed my list about the webinar, posted on Facebook, and told my entrepreneur friends and current clients, hoping that at least 100 people would show up to the webinar.

Three people showed up live and only five registered. For a split second I was deflated, but a little voice inside of me said pretend you have a packed house and give it your all. I taught the workshop I outlined, answered questions, and helped people figure out their offerings. After about 45 minutes, I made them an offer to work with me privately.

According to WebinarNinja, seeing 15 percent of live attendees purchase a product or sign up for a trial is a decent conversion rate.[22] That meant for me to sign one new client from my webinar, I would have needed at least seven people to show up live, and possibly more, since I was enrolling people in a $3,000-plus package.

I didn't even have seven people register for the webinar. That being said, two out of the three attendees signed up to become private clients after booking a sales call from that webinar. That one webinar generated over $5,000 in revenue. If statistically I needed seven people to make one sale, how did I make two with just three people? I believe it's because I knew who my offer was perfect for, gave them the option to solve their problem with me at their side, and gave them a taste of what that experience would be like.

YOUR TASTING SPOON

During my time in Portland, Oregon, I frequented Salt & Straw ice cream on NW 23rd Street, the closest location to my apartment. My first time there, I didn't know what I was in for. All I knew was that the line went out the door, so it had to be good. There were so many unique flavors: an olive oil flavor, a flavor with goat cheese, another one with lavender. Fortunately, Salt & Straw had a generous tasting spoon policy, and it eventually became one of my new favorite ice cream shops. Your business needs a tasting spoon.

You may have heard someone say that people buy from those they "know, like, and trust." But that's only part of the equation. A prospect also has to believe that you're the person or company that can help them achieve a desired result. That's why a tasting spoon is so important. An effective way to showcase the benefits and uniqueness of your product or service is by giving your prospect a trial run. If someone can test out your product or service and see the benefits firsthand, they're more likely to buy the product or service.

The concept of a tasting spoon can be applied to most industries. This is why you're able to try clothes on in stores, play with iPads at the Apple store, use software for a 14-day trial, or take advantage of a complimentary consultation before hiring a consultant.

Your goal is to provide prospective customers with such an amazing experience that they feel confident in purchasing your product or service. To give people a sense of what it would be like to be a part of my membership site, I deliver a free masterclass to allow prospective clients to experience how content is delivered inside my community.

Creating conversion events, such as webinars, masterclass series, demos, or a five-day or more challenge, can be an effective way of allowing potential customers to see for themselves what you're all about. After they utilize your offer, you can either invite them to buy from you right then and there, fill out an application for your program, or book a sales call to discover if working with you is a good fit.

To effectively convert leads into paying customers, you have to determine the most effective sequence of events to sell your product or service.

BUILDING A SALES SYSTEM

Once you've given someone a preview of what it's like to experience your product or service, it's time to walk them through a sequence of events that takes them from very interested to completed sale. The process by which you turn a lead into a customer is your sales system. At the highest level, your sales system may look like one of the following examples.

Example #1

- A prospective customer goes to your website and looks at a T-shirt.
- They look at pictures of other people wearing the T-shirt and read the reviews but leave your website without purchasing.
- Later, they see ads reminding them to buy your T-shirt (retargeting).
- Finally, they come back to your product page, put the T-shirt in their cart, and check out.

Example #2

- A prospective customer watches a demo of your software.
- They book a sales call to discover if your software is right for them.
- They show up to the sales call and decide to buy the software.
- Lastly, they receive and pay their invoice.

Example #3

- A prospective customer attends a masterclass series.
- They complete an application and book an enrollment call.
- Before the call, they receive a short video to watch.
- On the enrollment call, they say yes to the program and provide their credit card information over the phone.

To design a system that helps you turn prospects into customers, you must first answer the following three questions:

1. What does your prospect need to know in order to make the decision to buy your product/service or not buy your product/service?

   By understanding what your prospective customers need to know in order to say yes or no to your offer, you're able to decide how you will answer these questions before they get to your sales page.

   Here are examples of what your prospective customers may need to know before buying:

   - What your product is made of
   - What your product looks like
   - If the product or service will meet their needs
   - If other current customers recommend your product or service

   Before a sale can take place, you'll have to answer all of the questions running through your prospective customers' heads so they can choose to buy or not buy.

2. What does your prospect need to believe about your product/service to make the decision to buy your product/service or not buy your product/service?

   Earlier I stated that it's not just about knowing, liking, and trusting you. It's also about believing that your product or service can help them get a desired result. You'll need to go deeper into the beliefs your prospective client will need to have in order to say yes or no to your offer with ease.

Here are examples of what your prospective customers may need to believe before buying:

- Your offer is the type of solution they need for their problem.
- Your product or service can help them get a result.
- You are an expert in the industry.
- Your product or service is worth the investment.

The goal is to effectively communicate to your prospective client's inner voice that's debating if they should invest in your offer or not so they can make a decision with ease.

3. Who is the dream customer for your product or service, and what activities will help ensure you're attracting and working with your dream customer?

   This question is particularly important if you have a service-based business and work privately with your clients or if you are curating a community.

   By answering this question, you'll determine if you need an application or screening call as part of your sales system or if you will allow people to buy directly from your website without any prerequisite.

   Here are examples of what you may use to qualify dream customers:

   - Problem they're looking to solve
   - Level of urgency to solve problem
   - Stage of business
   - Coachability

> If a prospective client is interested in your product but does not meet your dream client qualifications, you can state that working together will not be a good fit and even refer them to other programs that might be.

By answering these three questions, you'll be able to design your sales system. Building the system is only half of the equation. Once you have a plan, implementing it is the next step, and the success of your implementation begins with your sales mindset.

A NEW SALES PERSPECTIVE

When I talk to people about sales, I receive a lot of reactions.

"I hate sales" or "I don't want to come off as super salesy and sleazy" are two of the most common comments I hear. If you are having those thoughts, know that you're not alone.

If you want to have consistent revenue in your business, sales will need to become your new best friend. And loving sales, or at least not completely hating it, begins with your mindset.

Whether you realize it or not, you're selling something every day. In fact, I sold a friend on the idea of watching *Knives Out* when it was in theaters.

Sales doesn't mean convincing somebody to buy something they don't need or pressuring somebody to buy something they don't want. Sales is offering a product, service, or idea to someone who is looking to solve a problem or realize a dream.

When *Knives Out* was in theaters, I was speaking to a friend who wanted to go to a movie with her husband. We spoke for a little while about the types of movies she liked and what types of movies her husband liked. After knowing their preferences, I thought they would love *Knives Out* as much as

I did. I recommended the movie and shared why they would love the movie without discussing the plot.

Selling your product or service is like selling someone on the idea of seeing a movie. It's understanding what a person really needs and wants so you can make a recommendation you believe will be great for them. In many ways, sales is a form of service. When a person is effective at sales, it's a win-win for everyone involved.

SETTING YOURSELF UP FOR THE SALE

Before you can make an offer, you have to believe in your offer. The level in which you believe in your offer is the level in which you'll be able to effectively sell your offer. If you're not confident that your product or service will make an amazing difference in the lives of your customers, then you won't be able to confidently make an offer.

To get ready for your sales activities, I recommend that you create a routine that gets you out of your own head so you can focus on your prospective customer. Here are three of my favorite activities to help you get ready for your sales activities.

The F*cking Fabulous List™

One of the exercises that I have people do is what I call the F*cking Fabulous List, also known as the freaking fabulous list. This is a list of all the reasons why you and your offer are freaking fabulous. Essentially you're asking the questions "Why would my ideal client or customer love this?" and "What is amazing about this offer?"

Going back to *Knives Out*, when I recommended it the first time, I was so energetic about it. The experience was fresh in my mind. As time went by, I remembered I loved it and I still recommended it, but my energy wasn't the same. It wasn't reinvigorated until I saw the movie again on Amazon Prime.

This could be happening with your offers. If you're not reminding yourself why it's freaking fabulous, you may not be fully expressing its value to your prospective customers.

This is why I recommend either rereading or rewriting your F*cking Fabulous List before selling or marketing your product. The goal is to constantly reconnect with why your offer is amazing.

The Perfect Fit

Believing in your offer can help you during the sales process, but it's not the only factor that's important. You also need to consider your prospective customers' wants and needs.

Have you met someone who believed in a product, service, or experience so strongly that they kept trying to get you to join even though it wasn't a right fit for you? Maybe you said, "I'm happy you're happy," then prayed they would stop trying to get you to be as interested or excited.

You should believe your product or service is freaking fabulous but also get clear on *who* it's fabulous for.

For example, I have a friend who loves horror movies. If there's a new scary movie in theaters, she's there. It brings her joy to watch these types of movies. But while we may have conversations about if she liked the latest fear-inducing film and if she found it scary, she knows never to invite me to a truly scary movie with her. The idea of going to a scary movie gives me nightmares. However, if she saw a great murder mystery, a superhero movie, or an action movie, she'd invite me in a heartbeat. When you consistently visualize who your product or service is perfect for and why, you'll not only believe that your offer is freaking fabulous, you'll also remember that while it's amazing, it might not be for everyone. Knowing who your offering is and isn't for will make you better at sales.

The Inner Soundtrack Remix

The biggest obstacle you'll face in the sales process is your mind.

I used to think that if I attended a transformational seminar or read a mindset book, my inner critic would be gone forever. But transforming your thoughts is a continuous journey. Fears, doubts, and concerns are bound to arise throughout your life and especially during the sales process. When you have negative thoughts as you're about to get on a sales call or write copy for your sales page, one of the best things you can do is disrupt the thoughts.

To be present during the sales process, you have to check your fears at the door.

To help me disrupt my own disempowering thoughts, I created a process called the inner soundtrack remix.

If you've ever had a song stuck in your head, you'll be able to master this fun yet powerful tool for disrupting your thoughts. The idea is to have a set of songs at the ready to empower you and pump you up when you need them.

Personally, I like songs where the lyrics are words I need to feel and believe in the process. Sia's "Unstoppable" and "The Greatest" are examples of songs that I play, sing out loud, and even dance to before hopping on sales calls. When I'm singing about how I'm unstoppable, invincible, or the greatest, my disempowering thoughts disappear, even if it's just for the duration of the sales activity.

Find a song or create a playlist of songs you can listen to before your sales activities so you check your disempowering thoughts at the door and feel empowered and in the zone when you're selling.

PLAY BY PLAY FOR A POWERFUL SALES CONVERSATION

I like to approach sales as if I'm a doctor doing a consultation.

When you go to the doctor's office, they look at your test results and ask you a lot of questions to determine what, if any, health issues you have. Then they give you a recommendation for treatment, walk you through how it would work, and allow you to choose for yourself if that's the way you want to go or not.

Selling a product or service via a sales call is similar to this process. Depending on your product, this consultation could be completed in one call, or it could be a two-call process. In this section, I'm going to walk you through the stages of a sales conversation so you can decide for yourself if a one- or two-call strategy is right for you.

Getting on the Same Page

Take a moment and picture yourself walking into a dealership to buy a car. What are the thoughts that immediately come to mind? At the beginning of a sales call, your prospective client may be a little tense or resistant. They most likely go into the experience with their own preconceived thoughts, just as you would at a car dealership.

That's why at the beginning of the conversation, I recommend you lay out how the conversation will go so you're both on the same page and at ease.

Here's an example of how the beginning of a conversation could go:

> **You**: Hi, Julia! Is now still a good time for you?
>
> **Julia**: It is!

You: Great. I like to start these conversations by walking you through what you can expect. Is that a good place to start for you?

Julia: Yes, thank you.

You: Perfect. For a large portion of this call, I'll ask you a lot of questions. My intention is to truly understand where you are and what your goals are so I can provide you with a recommendation that's specific to you. Then once I have a clear picture of where you are and what your goals are, I'll provide you with my recommendation. If the recommendation is of interest to you, I'll walk you through how it would work and answer any questions so you can make a decision to move forward working with me or not. If during our conversation, I realize that what I offer would not be a fit for you, we'll discuss some recommendations I have for others in my industry so I can refer you to someone who could be a great fit. How does that sound?

Julia: That sounds great. Thank you.

By walking your prospective customer through the conversation before it happens, you help quiet their questions about how the conversation is going to go so they can be present while you two converse.

Getting Curious

Once you're on the same page with your prospective customer about how the conversation is going to go, you'll want to discover what life is like for them right now in the area you help people with. If you're all about helping people with their businesses, you want to get a real understanding of what their business is like. If you're helping people with love, get inside their love life and their world. You want to be able to understand not just how their love life looks but how it's impacting all other areas of their life.

We have two ears and one mouth for a reason.

In this getting curious phase, you want to discover the answers to the following questions:

- What's their big dream or vision?
- What is their 90-day or 12-month goal?
- Why haven't they achieved their goal yet?
- Is there a problem? If so, what is the problem?
- What are the symptoms of the problem?
- Why are they having this sales conversation now? Are they ready to make a change or are they just testing the waters?
- What have they already tried to solve the problem?

You want to truly understand why they have been unable to do the thing they want so badly without making them feel wrong or broken because of it. It's purely about being curious from a judgment-free zone and getting into their world.

A great way to get answers to these questions is to ask open-ended questions and follow up with phrases like "Tell me more," "Why do you think that is?" or "Have you experienced something similar in other areas of your life as well?"

You've done your job when you've asked questions in such a way that your potential client starts realizing for themselves what the real problem is. It might be exactly what they believe it is, or it might be something deeper. For example, let's say a person books a call with you because they want to lose weight and they think their problem is accountability. During the call, you both discover that they are actually afraid to be objectified at work if they look the way they used to. As a result, you can now recommend a program or person who can best help them based on their real roadblock.

During the curiosity phase, resist the urge to be a cheerleader or talk about how you've been exactly where they are. You're there purely to get inside their world and understand what they want and need to get there.

Recap the Discoveries

Once you have a clear picture of what your prospective client wants and what their life is like, it's time to do a brief recap of the curiosity phase to ensure everyone is aligned on the goal and the current roadblocks.

This part of the conversation could sound like this:

> **You:** If it's all right with you, Julia, I'm going to quickly recap what we've discussed so far to make sure I have everything right.
>
> **Julia:** That works.
>
> **You:** Your big goal is to lose 50 pounds this year so you can be more active with your children and be a healthy example and role model for them. You grew up in a household with unhealthy habits and want to provide a different environment for your family. Because you're trying to do everything at work and at home by yourself, you've been having a hard time planning and preparing healthy meals for your family and have gotten into the habit of buying whatever is quick and easy to make without looking at the nutritional value. You also realized that deep down you have a fear of losing the weight because when you

were 50 pounds lighter, you received a lot of inappropriate comments at work from your co-workers about your nice looks. In your dream scenario, one year from now, your family would be eating healthy meals together, you'd go on bike rides and play kickball together as a family, and you'd feel confident and strong in your own skin. Is there anything I missed?

Julia: That's exactly it!

Recapping the curiosity phase helps your prospective customer know that you truly understand where they are right now. If you understand their world, you're more likely to be able to help them.

Show That You've Helped People Just Like Them

After you've made it clear that you understand where they are and where they want to go, it's important to show them that you have experience helping people just like them solve the same problems.

You may use this time to say something like the following:

You: The first thing I want you to know, Julia, is that you're not alone. I've helped over 50 mothers who felt burnt out and uncomfortable in their skin lose 50 pounds or more. In fact, just last week I had a client officially hit the 75-pound weight-loss milestone. She had been so focused on being a rock star at work and at home that she forgot to take care of herself and found herself frustrated and sad that she couldn't keep up with her kids when they were playing outside. For the past 10 months, we've been increasing her knowledge of foods so she could make better decisions at the grocery store, creating new habits so she could prepare healthier meals in advance, and trying out new physical activities that keep her motivated and moving. In fact, she's just taken on kickboxing.

Julia: Oh my gosh, I would love to do something like that.

You: It's absolutely possible for you, Julia.

Provide a Recommendation

Once you've shown that you can help your prospective customer get their desired results either by using a client as a case study or by sharing what you've personally accomplished, it's time to give your recommendation.

When giving a recommendation, I like to keep it to no more than three specific things someone would need to work on so they are not left confused or overwhelmed by my suggestions. In fact, I recommend that you have a list of 5 to 10 specific things you help your customers with so you can choose the top three for each prospective customer's needs.

The key is to share what you recommend they focus on and the benefits of focusing on each area. A great phrase to use is "so that." It would look like this:

You: Based on everything we've discussed, if we were to work together, we'd start with creating a meal-planning and preparation habit so that you can eat healthier meals consistently, even on days where you have to run out the door quickly. While we're developing the habit of meal planning, we'll also search for activities you enjoy. By trying new things, we'll be able to pinpoint what types of exercise you'll find fun and enjoyable.

Julia: This sounds exactly like what I need. I'd love to find exercises I find fun and exciting.

The Invitation

Once you've shared your recommendation with your prospective client, you can ask them if they have any questions so far. If they ask you how they can work with you, you can go right into making an offer. If they either don't have any questions or their questions are not about working together, you can answer the questions they do have then ask them if they'd like to discuss what it would look like to work together.

Once they say yes, your job is to give them an idea of what it would be like to work with you. Avoid giving them every little detail. Going back to the movie example, if someone wants to know what a movie is about before they see it, they don't want spoilers; they want a general plot description.

You want to do the same here. It could sound something like this:

> **You:** I work with clients for a 12-month period. In the first 30 days, we'd work on building new eating habits and moving more so you can lose the first five pounds or more and start getting momentum. Then once we've started to develop new habits, we're going to spend the next 30 days working specifically on your exercise routine so you are working out at least five days a week. By the end of the first 90 days, you will have developed new habits and routines that will help you consistently lose five to eight pounds a month for the first four months. Then once you get close to your target weight, we'll work on switching up your plan to break through any plateaus. Once you hit your goal weight, we'll work on maintenance so you do not gain back the weight you've lost. Does this sound like a fit for you?

Julia: Yes, this is exactly what I was looking for!

You: Great, do you have any questions for me before we talk about the next steps and how to get started?

Note: I am not a health coach, doctor, nutritionist, or personal trainer, so I'm making up these recommendations for demonstration purposes only.

Once your prospective client has said yes to your program or offer, you can move forward with sharing the price if you haven't already and walk them through the options for payment and any next steps.

While the examples shared in this section were for a conversation, you can also use the flow to write your sales page or make an offer at the end of a conversion event, such as a webinar or masterclass series.

The goal is twofold: For your prospective customer, it's to help them determine if your program is right for them or not. For you, it's to determine if you can and want to help your prospective customer reach their goals.

Remember, the sales process is no different than selling someone on the idea of seeing a great movie with you. You have to get to know them, understand what they need and want, then make a recommendation and an offer.

IMPLEMENTATION CHECKLIST

Before moving on to the next chapter, make sure you have completed these action steps:

- ❑ Map out your sales system.
- ❑ Create your F*cking Fabulous List.
- ❑ Choose a pre-sales conversation song or ritual.

- [ ] Head to marketyourgeniusbook.com/chapter7 to access worksheets, my playlist, and interviews with sales experts.

Over the past three chapters, we've mapped out a plan for generating qualified leads and turning those leads into customers. In the next chapter, we'll discuss how to validate your plan so you can use it to consistently create new customers.

CHAPTER 8

TEST LIKE A M.A.A.D. SCIENTIST

"Be bold. If you're going to make an error, make it a doozy, and don't be afraid to hit the ball."

— Billie Jean King, LGBTQ advocate and former #1 professional tennis player with 39 grand slam titles[23]

That's it! I quit! I've been posting these videos online seemingly forever and I'm pretty sure nobody cares!

At least once a week I'd have to talk myself out of jumping off the "never gonna do content marketing again" cliff.

It all started when I woke up one morning with what I believed was a brilliant idea. I was going to start a Facebook live show called *Content & Coffee.*

I've always wanted to have a TV show, and while I didn't see myself becoming the next Kelly Ripa anytime soon, I felt like I could at least get comfortable on camera by dropping some content marketing knowledge every week for current and aspiring entrepreneurs.

Every morning I'd wake up, turn on the lighting system that my old co-workers had graciously set up in my Boston apartment, and film an episode of my newly formed show, *Content & Coffee*.

Despite going live on a regular basis and sharing what I thought was game-changing advice, I didn't feel like it made an actual dent in my business.

Day after day, I'd go live, and my client base never seemed to surge.

After a while I started to drop off from doing *Content & Coffee*. Daily became weekly, then weekly became gone forever. Almost as quickly as it had started, *Content & Coffee* ceased to exist. I continued to do Facebook lives and share valuable business information, but I only went live randomly.

Months after dropping *Content & Coffee*, people started reaching out to me via Facebook Messenger, asking if I could help them with their marketing strategy.

> "I used to watch all of your videos and I finally feel ready for some 1:1 support."

> "I need help with my content plan and I heard you're the person I need to speak to."

> "I just found one of your videos on how to map out a content plan in 30 minutes or less, and it was so incredibly helpful."

It turns out all of those videos I thought nobody was watching actually had a fan base. Many of them never liked, commented, or shared one darn video, but in their eyes, I was the expert when it came to marketing. Those videos helped me sign clients that paid upwards of $10,000 to work with me as their business consultant and marketing mentor.

If I set a goal for those videos, identified metrics, then captured and reviewed those metrics, I might have implemented strategies and tactics to have people engage with my videos. I might have realized how many people were watching the videos and maybe even the duration they watched them. If I had the metrics, I might not have given up so quickly.

But living in the might-nots or might-have-beens doesn't serve anyone.

It's about learning and evolving.

If I've learned one thing about entrepreneurship, it's that collecting and looking at data gives you insight into what's actually happening in your business versus what you think is happening.

I've spoken to many entrepreneurs who have said, "I don't know what's going wrong. I don't understand why my business isn't working." Then we look at their numbers and the picture becomes clear.

Know your numbers!

IMPLEMENTATION FOR INFORMATION

One thing I've become great at as an entrepreneur is being able to fail with a combination of self-proclaimed grace, tremendous curiosity, and unrelenting humor.

When I jumped into entrepreneurship, I had no idea that the majority of my job would be to metaphorically fall off the bike and get back on. No one told me that building a business is one giant science experiment.

You won't know the "thing" that is going to work for you until you've tried "things" that don't work.

In love, they say you have to kiss a lot of toads before finding your prince or princess.

Business is the same.

In fact, when it comes to business, you have to kiss a lot of pavement before you can afford the reconstructive surgery your face will need after falling so damn much.

You have to keep trying and trying to learn what works and doesn't work until things work out the way you've always dreamed. Each time you try, you discover more about what does and doesn't work for you until you finally nail it.

As an entrepreneur, you're going to make mistakes.

You're going to fail at something. And to be realistic, you're going to fail at many things.

That's really the beauty of the journey.

GET YOUR MIND READY, IT'S GONNA HURT

The University College London conducted a study where groups of volunteers received an electric shock on the back of the hand. Some knew they were definitely going to get the electric shock while others simply knew it was a possibility. The study researchers found that the stress response was higher for those who only knew that the shock was a possibility.[24]

Said another way, it's the not knowing that induces the stress response.

In building a business, you're going to have failures.

Something is not going to work out.

But when you let the fear of the unknown take over your actions, you will end up stressed and more likely to make a mistake.

Why not embrace the fact that something will inevitably go wrong? This allows you to enjoy the science experiment that comes with entrepreneurship and learn from the errors that come your way.

If you're already well into your entrepreneurial journey and are still holding onto mistakes you've made, let them go.

I could argue that I wasted over $100K as a result of the mistakes that I made while building my business, but the truth is it was just part of my journey to get where I am today.

Sh*t happens. But make sure you use it to shift something within you so you come out on the other side stronger, better, and faster.

I'm pretty sure that last part sounded like a Nike commercial and I'm cool with that.

RUN YOUR BUSINESS LIKE A M.A.A.D. SCIENTIST

I believe that building a business is one giant market experiment.

You can figure out what works in your business by coming up with a hypothesis and testing it out.

Let's take a look at something millions of people use every day, the light bulb. If you google how many experiments Thomas Edison did while trying to bring a commercially acceptable light bulb to the world, you'll get a wide range of answers.[25]

That being said, I read a Rutgers University newsletter that directed me to a letter addressed to Edison in 1884.[26] In this letter, Francis Upton stated that the lamp factory had conducted 2,774 experiments to date.[27] These 2,774 experiments took place after 6,000 different materials were tested solely to find a filament. That means they failed at least 2,774 times before they created a light bulb that was commercially acceptable. And 6,000 times before that just to find a filament.

Treat failure like a scientist.

For many scientists and inventors, failure is just one more piece of information that leads you closer to the answer.

It all starts with a hypothesis, a theory on how to make something happen.

Want more leads? Then what is your theory on how to make that a reality?

CREATING YOUR HYPOTHESIS

At the end of the second year of owning my business, I had a goal to focus on fewer things. I strongly believed I could get further by simplifying my business.

At the time I was offering at least five different products and services that were all similar in content: 90-day packages, six-month packages, three-hour sessions, a mini course, and 90-minute intensives. I even had some done-for-you services that I offered for select clients.

I was so afraid that no one would buy from me that I tried to make it so that no matter the budget, I had a product.

Unfortunately, as a one-person shop that only had a part-time virtual assistant, I was overwhelmed.

Despite an effort to make myself available regardless of price, there wasn't one offer that sold drastically differently from another. In the same time period that five people purchased my $497 product, three people purchased my $5,000 product. Yet both of them required my time.

I was burning out, and quite honestly, I wasn't even sure if I was doing anything at the level that I wanted to.

So I came up with the following hypothesis: "I believe I can make more money and make a bigger impact by only offering one product and by focusing on speaking and live video to acquire clients."

I streamlined everything I did. If it wasn't related to those activities, I didn't do it.

As a result, I more than doubled my average monthly income in less than four months, and I created deeper relationships with our clients.

I stopped trying a different tactic every month and stuck with a simple game plan.

When you look online, there is no shortage of different methods for generating leads and clients. Webinars; challenges; networking events; speaking on stages; being interviewed on podcasts, video series, and live launches; connecting with people on LinkedIn; using Instagram, Facebook, TikTok—the list goes on.

For a long time, I jumped from method to method, half implementing each one before I got excited about a "new opportunity" or a "new way of doing things."

The truth is most of these marketing tactics work. At the very least, they've worked for someone.

The key is to find out what will work for *you*. I recommend that you create a hypothesis for the best way to consistently have your target audience buy your product(s) and test that hypothesis.

I use the M.A.A.D. Scientist Method™ to do this. The M.A.A.D. Scientist Method is a process I designed to help clients systematically test their marketing, sales, or business plans. It's an acronym that stands for **M**ap It Out (your hypothesis); **A**ctivate the plan; **A**djust the plan (based on your results); and **D**o it again with the necessary changes.

THE M.A.A.D. SCIENTIST FRAMEWORK

This four-step method is all about testing your hypothesis over and over again, each time adjusting a variable (or a few) to get closer to the desired result.

You can believe that webinars, live videos, networking events, and podcast interviews will help you grow your business. But to know for sure, you have to test it.

Implementation leads to information. Let's walk through each step in a bit more detail.

Step 1: Map It Out

My initial hypothesis was that I could make more money and make a bigger impact by only offering one product and focusing on signing clients through speaking and live video.

While that was a general direction, the first step was to map it out in a detailed game plan.

Mapping out your game plan helps you better evaluate what you do and the results you get more effectively.

Your game plan (or profit plan, as I like to call it) should consist of the following:

- What you want to be known for and the problem you solve (Chapter 2)
- The target audience for your genius (Chapter 3)
- The offer(s) your target audience demands (Chapter 4)
- How you'll generate leads (Chapter 5)
- How you'll nurture your leads (Chapter 6)
- How you'll convert your leads into customers (Chapter 7)

Advanced plans will also include:

- How you'll turn your customers into raving fans (Chapter 9)
- How you'll generate a consistent flow of referrals (Chapter 10)
- How you'll create clients for life (Chapter 11)

The key to this step is to resist the urge to be perfect, to be okay with not getting it perfect, and to not overthink it. The best source of information will come from implementation.

The entire point of the M.A.A.D. Scientist Method is to test and validate everything you put into your game plan so you can adjust it.

You will not know what will or won't work until you try, so I encourage you to avoid aiming to create the perfect plan; I assure you, there's no such thing.

Step 2: Activate the Plan

Having a plan on paper is great, but putting it into practice is even better.

There are three things you have to do to rock this step:

1. Commit to the plan.
2. Understand the metrics you need to track in order to evaluate your plan.
3. Have a backup plan in case something goes wrong and you can't implement your initial plan at all.

Fully Committing

It's crucial that in activating your plan, you stick to it. You want to avoid rapidly switching your strategy or tactics. When you completely change the plan, you end up back in the Map It Out phase. You want to avoid getting stuck in the Map It Out stage. Again, think of it like a scientist. You want to come up with your hypothesis, map out your plan, and do the experiment. You will not know if your plan will work until you implement it.

Identifying Key Performance Indicators (KPIs)

When I stopped my *Content & Coffee* series, it's because I looked at two things: (1) the fact that I was going live on Facebook and (2) the fact that clients were not coming directly from my Facebook lives.

What was missing fell in between.

It is important to know what you need to measure in order to evaluate and improve your game plan.

One of my first jobs was at an ad agency. This is where I first heard the phrase *Key Performance Indicator (KPI)*. KPIs are performance measurements that help people evaluate the effectiveness of their activities. I find them incredibly valuable to identifying if I'm on the right track when I'm working to accomplish a specific milestone or goal.

For example, if I wanted clients from my *Content & Coffee* series, I could have looked at the following measurements:

- Number of people that watched my videos
- Length of time people watched
- Percentage of people that liked, commented, and/or shared my video
- Percentage of people that booked a call with me from a video
- How many videos someone watched on average before booking a call

Taking the time to collect and evaluate this information could have helped me determine why I wasn't signing clients from my videos.

Track, know, and love your numbers.

To identify the metrics you should track and review, you can play a game I made up called "How Will I Know?"

I highly recommend playing Whitney Houston during this game, but it's not a rule.

Here is how to play "How Will I Know?":

1. Look at each piece of your game plan and ask yourself, *How will I know if this part of the game plan is successful?*
2. Look at everything you wrote down and ask yourself, *What metrics and data points can I collect that will indicate if I am on the right track?*

3. Review all of your data points and ask yourself, *What are the most important data points?* Then cross out anything that isn't necessary.
4. Create a chart to track and monitor these important metrics, then fill out the chart during your experiment.

Have a Backup Plan

In February 2020, I was working with a client on their signature workshop. The plan was to spend the year validating the in-person workshop and increasing the percentage of workshop attendees that became coaching clients over time.

One month later, all of my client's in-person speaking engagements were either postponed or canceled due to COVID-19.

If being an entrepreneur taught me anything, it's to be prepared for the unexpected.

As you map out your plan, ask yourself, *If something happens and I cannot do my plan the way I originally intended to, what would I do instead?*

For my client, we already had a plan for bringing her workshops and presentations online.

While you may not know what's coming next, it's a good practice to have a backup plan or a book of ideas you can pull from in the event of a crisis.

Step 3: Adjust Based on the Results

A year into my business, I had an idea for an amazing group program called the Bada$$ Coaches Academy (BCA). I was convinced it was everything a coach or consultant would need to generate a consistent flow of clients for their business.

I asked friends who were experts in their industry to do workshops. I watched big online personalities offer scholarships and early-bird discounts to their programs. So I tried to do the same.

No one purchased the program.

For a while I was so embarrassed that I didn't want to launch another group program ever again. And I was so defeated, I didn't take the time to look at my numbers to understand why the launch bombed.

Was it that I didn't have enough people in my audience?

Was it that it wasn't the right offer?

Was it that I was self-sabotaging?

Then I had a thought: *I can't be the only person this has happened to.* So I started connecting with some of my friends in the industry and guess what . . .

I wasn't the only one.

Review your results without judgment. The insights will help you improve your next attempt.

Step 4: Do It Again

When I launched my next group program, I did things differently. I wrote out and prescheduled emails to my audience. I personally messaged people in my audience that I thought would be a good fit. I tracked my results.

While I still missed my goal, I had four people enroll in this program, and I discovered how many people I really needed to connect with in order to sign a new client.

Persistence is your new secret weapon.

In that second launch, I was nervous and afraid. I had a fear of failure that I'm confident impacted my results.

But I did it anyway.

Knowing that I could keep trying again and again, improving each time, brought me some comfort. After a few months, I decided to proactively plan my experiments.

EXPERIMENT CYCLES

From my second launch to my fifth, I increased my revenue ten times over, reduced my stress, and took on clients I absolutely loved working with. With each launch, I felt more confident and comfortable with the process, and I learned more information and used it to improve the next experiment cycle. And as my results continued to improve, I started testing this system with clients.

Collectively, we've validated advertising campaigns, launched programs, multiplied sales numbers, landed speakerships, generated press, and written books.

We've made it normal to run our businesses like M.A.A.D. scientists.

To validate our hypotheses, we each choose one experiment to conduct eight times over a twelve-month period.

The process is the same each time:

1. Choose a goal.
2. Create a hypothesis.
3. Map out a game plan/action plan.
4. Implement the plan.
5. Review the results.
6. Adjust the plan.
7. Run the experiment again, cycling through Steps 4 to 7 throughout the year.

Map it out, take action, learn from that action, and do it again. While your results may not always be favorable, you'll definitely learn from them.

THE F WORD

In middle school, I loved the show *Daria*. If you're not familiar with the show, don't worry—it's not a prerequisite for what I'm about to share.

In season 4, episode 5, entitled "The 'F' Word," Mr. O'Neill, a high school teacher, was inspired by a motivational seminar he attended. He gives Daria and her fellow high school classmates an assignment: pick something they know they'll fail at and try to accomplish it anyway. The hope was that students would learn that failing was not the end of the world.

Essentially, he wanted his students to succeed at failing. Here is what some characters attempted:

- Brittany, a cheerleader, agreed to fail at being unpopular.
- Kevin, a quarterback for the football team, agreed to fail at being a bad athlete.
- Jodie, a high-achieving student, agreed to fail at trying to get the summer off as her parents overcommitted her to activities that would look good on her college applications.
- Mack, the only football player on the team with an above average GPA, agreed to fail at teaching Kevin the three branches of the American government.

At the end of the assignment, Jodie failed to convince her parents to let her take the summer off, and Mack failed to teach Kevin the three branches of government. Thus, they succeeded at the assignment.

Brittany ended up succeeding at being unpopular, leading her to be kicked off the cheerleading team, and Kevin played terribly at a football game on purpose, causing the team to lose and Kevin to be kicked off the team. Brittany and Kevin essentially failed at failing, but experiencing failure was the point of the assignment, so they received credit.

While Mr. O'Neill sent his students out to experience failure, he neglected to teach them how to move past it. After discovering that no one in the class left feeling proud of their failures, Mr. O'Neill ended up failing at teaching his students that it's okay to fail. And when he did, he ended up "slumped over his desk sobbing uncontrollably into his sweater belt."

In the end, Daria and her best friend Jane had to find Mr. O'Neill at his home and remind him that failing wasn't the end of the world. His students were not traumatized by the assignment and were able to resume life as if the experiment didn't take place. Even the person who set up this experiment needed to learn the lesson. Failure is not the end of the world.

Failure is an important part of the learning process that doesn't always feel good.

Similar to Mr. O'Neill, you may initially feel confident that you are going to be comfortable with failing while running your experiments. But reality might prove to be much harder than you initially thought. The key is to put systems and reminders in place to accept the failure and learn from it when it arises.

Here are some of my systems:

- I have messages on my office walls that say, "It's all just one giant science experiment" and "judgment-free zone."
- I allow myself to feel the failure and even cry but only for a certain period of time. Then I put on music and dance it out before going on a walk or a run.
- Once I've accepted the failure, I ask myself at least five times why I failed and write down what comes up. Then I use this information with the data I collected to determine what I'm going to tweak when I try again.

My ways may or may not work for you. Use the System for Resilience questionnaire in the next section to help you brainstorm a process to discover your system. The goal is to brainstorm different ways to not only get back on the horse when you fall off but also to evaluate without judgment why you fell off in the first place so you can stay on longer next time.

SYSTEM FOR RESILIENCE

1. Journal about something you failed at. How did it feel when you failed? What thoughts went through your mind?
2. How did your life change because of that failure? How do you feel about this change?
3. What are your beliefs about failure?
4. What thoughts or beliefs would leave you feeling empowered after a failure? How could you trigger these thoughts or beliefs after a failure?

5. What do you believe would help you feel non-judgmental and kind with yourself in the event of failure?

IMPLEMENTATION CHECKLIST

In this chapter, we discussed a strategy for validating your sales and marketing plan. In the next chapter, we'll discuss how to keep your new customers happy so they become your biggest advocates. Before moving on to the next chapter, make sure you have completed these action items:

- ☐ Review your sales and marketing plan.
- ☐ Identify your key performance indicators.
- ☐ Choose 6 to 12 experiment cycle periods for implementing your plan and put them on your calendar.
- ☐ Listen to the chapter's companion podcasts and access downloadable worksheets by heading to marketyourgeniusbook.com/chapter8.

PART III

HOW TO DELIVER YOUR GENIUS

In the "deliver" stage, your primary job is to provide such an amazing experience that your customers become raving fans. The ultimate goals are for customers to leave rave reviews, recommend you to their network, and become lifelong buyers.

Chapter 9: Reputation by Design. What your customers think about your offerings can make or break you. In this chapter, you'll:

- Discover what makes a quality customer experience so you can create a community of happy customers
- Learn how to evaluate your customer experience so you can improve it over time
- Explore ways to up-level your customer experience to stand out from competitors

Chapter 10: The (Social) Proof Is in the Pudding. Positive customer reviews and case studies make it easier for prospective customers to make buying decisions. In this chapter, you'll:

- Review the different types of social proof so you can determine what will work best for your business
- Create a plan for collecting and sharing customer results with prospective buyers
- Discover how social proof can impact your revenue and reputation

Chapter 11: Bring More A$$es in the Door. Studies show that people trust the recommendations of others over advertising. In this chapter, you'll:

- Discover what is (and what isn't) a referral so you can accurately track your results
- Outline your referral system so you can consistently generate leads from referrals
- Learn how to build referral relationships so your referral partners have all the information they need to send business your way

Chapter 12: Clients 4 Life. Keeping customers is just as important as attracting new ones. In this chapter, you'll:

- Explore ways to increase the lifetime value of your customers
- Learn how to seed the idea of a long-term relationship before a customer makes their first purchase
- Build your Clients 4 Life System so you have a road map for keeping customers year after year

CHAPTER 9

REPUTATION BY DESIGN

"Succeed to serve."

— Sung-Joo Kim, a visionary and global business leader who was once disowned by her family for going after her dream of a career in the Western fashion industry

During my time in corporate America, I used to hear some of my co-workers say, "Happy wife, happy life."

When I started my business, that sentence kept playing in my head. Only instead of "wife," it would be "customer" or "client."

Happy customer, happy life.

Happy client, happy life.

Unfortunately, neither "customer" nor "client" rhyme with "life," and I have yet to come up with a sentence that gets that point across and rhymes.

If you do, please shoot me an email at books@nikkinash.co and I'll share my favorites on one of my social platforms. I can't wait to hear what you've come up with.

Your business dies or thrives based on its reputation.

A Global Customer Experience Benchmarking Report found that 84 percent of companies that worked to improve their customer experience saw an increase in their revenue.[28]

One of the most important jobs your business will have is meeting, and ideally exceeding, customer expectations. When your customers are happy, they are more likely to leave positive reviews, refer your business, and continue to buy from you.

CUSTOMER EXPERIENCE BY DESIGN

Consistently creating happy customers doesn't just happen. It happens by design. Systems and structures must be put in place to ensure that every customer has the same amazing experience.

Think about the last item you purchased. What was your experience like? Was it enjoyable or frustrating? If they messed up, how did they resolve the problem? Would you buy from them again?

Think about the last time you made an appointment somewhere. Was the person that answered the phone friendly or rude? Were they helpful?

Every interaction your customer has with your brand shapes their perspective of your business. That's why it is important to create systems and guidelines for interacting with current and prospective customers.

There are five steps to consistently create a positive experience for your customers. They are the five Cs:

Create a plan for your customer experience.

Collect customer feedback.

Catalog and synthesize their feedback into actionable steps.

Complete action steps identified as a priority.

Communicate updates with your customers.

The five Cs process is a continuous loop that is designed to help your business consistently deliver a superior customer experience.

Step 1: Creating a Happy Customer Game Plan

It all starts with building your "happy customer game plan."

The goal is to create a plan that leaves your customers saying, "OMG, using this product was so easy," or "They thought of everything; this was such a smooth experience."

To create a plan, I like to pretend I am the customer buying my product or service. I close my eyes and picture everything from the moment they hit the checkout button to them writing a rave review. Then I write down everything that is needed to deliver that amazing experience.

Here are examples of questions you could ask yourself to map out your initial customer experience plan:

Initial Communication

- When a customer hits CHECKOUT or pays an invoice, how will I acknowledge their purchase or payment?
- Will they be redirected to a thank you page? If so, what will be on the page?
- Will they get an email? What will the email say? What information do they need immediately?
- If something is being shipped, how will they get the tracking information?

- Do they need product onboarding or training? If so, what needs to happen to successfully onboard a customer?
- If they need a password, how will they receive or create it?
- Do they need to complete a welcome packet or an assessment?
- What are the immediate next steps for the customer after purchase?

Product or Service Use

- What information does the customer need in order to get results from the product or service? How will that information be delivered to them?
- How can a customer ask questions or get support if needed?
- Who will manage customer support? What are the customer support hours?
- What are the current or anticipated frequently asked questions (FAQs)? What are the answers?
- How do I want customers to feel when they engage with customer support?
- What are the customer support guidelines?

Feedback

- How will I know if customers are happy?
- How will I work with an unhappy customer?
- How will I get feedback from customers?
- How will I use that feedback to improve the customer experience?

Step 2: Collect Customer Feedback

The only way you can deliver an experience that people want to tell their friends about is to get a report card from your customers—their rating of your game plan and your success in implementing it.

Putting a system in place to get feedback allows you to quickly address any issues and improve your customer experience. This allows you to create happy clients and convert them into raving fans.

Let's dive into two ways you can get feedback from your customers.

Net Promoter Score

Have you ever received an email from a company that asked, "On a scale from 1 to 10, how likely is it that you would recommend this product to a friend or colleague?" If so, you've seen the Net Promoter Score®, aka NPS®, in action.

NPS is a common method to determine if you are meeting or exceeding customer expectations. It was created by Fred Reichheld, a partner at Bain & Company, and is used by companies around the world.[29]

A Net Promoter Score measures the customer's experience and predicts business growth. It's based on asking your customers one question:

> "On a scale from 1 to 10, how likely is it that you would recommend [insert your brand/product/service] to a friend or colleague?"

Then the customer has the option to share their rationale for their rating.

Once a customer answers the question, they're grouped into one of three categories:

> Promoters (score 9–10): Loyal enthusiasts who will keep buying and will refer others, fueling growth

Passives (score 7–8): Customers who are "satisfied for now." They are less likely to repurchase and refer your business than promoters and are more likely to switch to a competitor if a competitor's offer catches their eye.

Detractors (score 0–6): Unhappy customers whose experience could negatively impact your brand. They often account for over 80 percent of a business's negative word of mouth.

Asking customers to complete the survey is only part of the process. To see how your company is doing month over month or quarter over quarter, you must calculate your total Net Promoter Score.

A company's total Net Promoter Score is the percentage of promoters minus the percentage of detractors.[30] For example, if a company's results are 65 percent promoters and 10 percent detractors, their NPS would be 55. When you track your NPS over periods of time, you will be able to determine if you are improving your customers' experience.

According to data from Bain & Company, companies with the highest NPS in their industry tend to outgrow their competitors by at least two times.[31]

Listening

While NPS can help you evaluate the happiness of your customers, you can also get feedback by reading ratings and online reviews, analyzing customer service reports for common issues, or conducting quick feedback calls midway and after your program.

Your goal is to get real-time feedback from customers about their experience so you can make improvements.

Step 3: Catalogue and Synthesize Feedback

When I started my business, I conducted sessions with clients over the phone. During one session, a client requested that we do calls via video conference instead. She thought it would be easier to talk through business concepts if we could see each other's face.

Intrigued by the idea, I sent a poll to all of my clients and asked who would like to switch our sessions from phone calls to video conferences. Every single client requested video.

Within days, I went from doing every session over the phone to video conference calls. In addition to seeing each other's faces, we were able to record sessions and share our screens. This small change dramatically increased the happiness of my clients and the value they received.

Getting feedback from your customers is only part of the equation. The next step is to aggregate and analyze the feedback to determine what improvements need to be made.

I recommend that you review feedback and update your customer happiness plan once a quarter at a bare minimum. The key with feedback is to identify common issues, questions, requests, and patterns, then create and prioritize your response.

Here are some questions you could ask to evaluate feedback:

- What questions or requests are most frequently asked?
- Are these questions or requests that have been asked before? If so, is it now more or less frequently asked?
- Are there common reasons why people are contacting support?
- Where are people getting stuck in their customer journey?

- Are there common frustrations or issues?
- How is our overall rating versus the last period? Is it improving, declining, or remaining the same?
- What is our customer retention rate? Is this improving, declining, or remaining the same?

To keep it simple, put all customer feedback into one master spreadsheet then color-code common questions, comments, and requests in order to identify patterns. For example, every time someone leaves a comment or a question about how they're not sure when a group call is, we make note of it by giving their comment a specific color.

You'll likely find that some feedback will be similar, although there may be some outliers. I recommend making a list of all the feedback then ranking it so you can prioritize your next steps. For example, if we see that the color assigned to not knowing the time of group calls takes up a lot of the spreadsheet, we may conclude that this is a common challenge and put it high on the priorities list.

Step 4: Complete Priority Action Steps

Depending on the size of your team and the complexity of the feedback, you may only be able to address three to seven issues in a 90-day period.

After ranking feedback, I recommend that you start with your top three and allocate time with team members to brainstorm solutions for each problem. If you do not have a team, this could be something you do with your business consultant or business bestie.

Then choose a solution and create an implementation plan.

With many of our customers having a hard time remembering the date, time, and dial-in information for our group calls, we brainstormed the following list:

- Send emails one hour before each call.
- Send text messages 20 minutes before each call.
- Put the call on everyone's calendar.
- Add a calendar of the calls on the homepage of our membership site.
- Tag people in reminders about the group call inside the Facebook group.

Take the time to brainstorm solutions for a customer service challenge that you have. Once you decide on the tactics you will implement, it's time to ask the following questions:

- Who is responsible for this action?
- Is this a one-time assignment or a recurring assignment?
- When is the deadline?
- Is anyone else involved in implementing this solution? If so, what is their role?
- What other deadlines must be reached to implement this solution?
- How will the team keep track of these steps and deadlines?
- How will you know if this solution was successful?

Then you or someone on your team can create a project management plan to ensure that everything gets done. You can use tools, such as Monday, Asana, Basecamp, Airtable, or Trello, to manage your business projects.

To see how we use project management templates internally, head to marketyourgeniusbook.com/project-management.

Step 5: Communicate Updates with Customers

Once you've determined your solution and have created your action plan, it's time to update your customers. Feeling heard is a key component of customer happiness. If your customers take the time to give you feedback, please take the time to show them that you appreciate their comments and are taking them to heart.

Here's what your customers want to know:

- That you received their feedback
- That you're working on their requests, comments, and concerns
- Which requests you're currently working on and approximately when they can expect to see the solution implemented
- That you're continuing to address comments and concerns and appreciate them taking the time to give you feedback

Communication is the key to a healthy relationship with your customers. If you can show them what's coming and even allow them to beta test new features, they'll feel connected to your business and will be less likely to switch to another brand.

HOW TO UP-LEVEL YOUR CUSTOMER HAPPINESS PLAN

Picture yourself going into a coffee shop. When you walk up to the counter, the barista asks you how you are and what you would like to order. They answer all of your questions with a smile then put your order into their point-of-sale system (POS). A price comes up on the screen, and when you tap your phone against the screen, your order is immediately paid for and you are given reward points. The barista lets you know that your order will be ready at the end of the counter in about two minutes.

When you walk to the end of the counter, you see another smiling barista calling people's names, handing customers their orders, and wishing them a wonderful day. After a minute, the barista calls your name and lets you know that the muffin you ordered is coming fresh out of the oven and it just needs another two minutes to cool down. While you stand there, you notice that everyone behind the counter seems approachable, friendly, and available if you need them.

After two more minutes, your name is called and you are handed a fresh muffin, a coffee, and napkins. The person behind the counter shows you where you can find sugar and asks if there is anything else they can help you with. Since you don't need anything, they wish you a wonderful day and out the door you go.

You leave the coffee shop feeling amazing and find yourself recommending this coffee shop to everyone you know. Not only was the service amazing, your coffee and muffin were absolutely delicious.

Your customers will remember an overwhelmingly positive experience, but even more so, an overwhelmingly poor one.

In addition to the five Cs, there are five more elements you should consider before you have customers to ensure they have an amazing experience. They were depicted in the coffee shop story, and I'll break them down for you now.

1. Tone and Vibe

The tone and vibe of everything you and your team say and do impacts the customer experience. All it takes is for one person to be rude to a customer on the phone to create a negative experience. In the coffee shop story, this was depicted by the way you were greeted when you arrived. Specifically, the barista asked you how you were and what you would like to order. They then answered all of your questions with a smile. At the end, a different barista directed you to the sugar, asked if there was anything else they could do for you, and wished you a wonderful day.

Guidelines and systems help you ensure a consistent tone and vibe with every customer.

Here are examples of how a company can ensure a consistent tone and vibe:

- Sharing company values before hiring
- Creating and sharing a customer experience standard operating procedure (SOP) guide
- Collecting feedback from customers about each employee
- Rewarding positive customer experience ratings
- Providing customer service training

2. Simple Processes

Your business will likely have many systems, tools, processes, and software programs. The key is to have everything work seamlessly so that even complicated, behind-the-scenes systems are not felt by the customer. In the coffee shop story, one of the ways this was depicted was through the payment process. The barista put your order into their POS system. A price came up on the screen, you tapped your phone against the screen, and your order was immediately paid for and you were given reward points.

To ensure that your systems seem simple to your customers, take time to pretend to be your customer and see what the experience is like before and after a payment is made.

3. Communication

The more you communicate with your customers, the better. Think of the last time you purchased something online. How communicative was the company in letting you know when your order was processed, shipped, and delivered? Personally, I get incredibly frustrated when things do not arrive on time and I don't receive an email or phone call that it's delayed.

When a company is communicative, it creates a positive experience for customers. In the coffee shop story, before your order was due, a barista let you know that the muffin you ordered was coming fresh out of the oven and needed another two minutes to cool down. Then they completed your order before those additional two minutes were up.

To ensure consistent communication, your company needs to determine if communication will be automated, such as sending alerts about packages being shipped; manual, such as the barista calling out names and giving order updates; or hybrid, where some messages, like client onboarding emails, are automated and others, like sending a customized invoice, are manual.

As you walk through your customer's experience, ask where communication is needed and how it should be delivered. Then put these into automated, manual, or hybrid systems and structures so your customers are not left uninformed and unsatisfied.

4. Reachability

Not being able to get support when needed is incredibly frustrating for customers. This is often felt when the answer to a question is not listed anywhere on the product or website and there is a long customer service wait or there isn't a way to contact customer service at all. Determine how customers can reach you should there be a problem, and make that process clearly defined and easy to find. In the coffee shop story, while you were waiting for your coffee, you noticed that everyone behind the counter seemed approachable, friendly, and available if you needed them. A similar experience would be if you were at a retail store and you could easily identify and find someone who could help you by their uniform or name tags.

If you're running a service-based business, you may have a chat box on your website so people can ask questions, an email address for support, or a phone number people can use during customer service hours. To ensure you are reachable, identify the method by which customers can reach out to you and your target response time.

5. Personalization

When you can show your customers that you know their name and their history of calling or connecting with the company, it makes them feel special and important. In the coffee shop story, the barista called your name to update you on your order and again when they delivered your order.

When you keep track of your customers' orders, feedback, results, and birthdays, you're able to create personalized experiences, even if you are automating the process. For example, you may have a system that automatically emails your customers on their birthday and gives them a gift or a coupon. Or if someone is calling because of a recurring issue and if you have kept track of their previous complaints and what has been done to resolve them, you can then focus on different solutions if they are still having problems.

IMPLEMENTATION CHECKLIST

Building an amazing customer experience means putting yourself in your customers' shoes and improving their experience by listening to their feedback and making adjustments. In the next chapter, we'll discuss how to connect with customers that have a positive experience and build a system for collecting reviews and creating case studies. Before moving forward, make sure you complete these action items:

- ❑ Think about the last item you purchased or the last appointment you had. Did you have a positive experience? Note what stood out to you, good and bad.
- ❑ Take time to visualize an amazing customer experience for your dream customer. Write down everything you picture.
- ❑ Determine how you will collect and review feedback from your customers. Note how frequently you will complete this process.
- ❑ Head to marketyourgeniusbook.com/chapter9 to access the worksheets associated with this chapter.

CHAPTER 10

THE (SOCIAL) PROOF IS IN THE PUDDING

"Create 'Team You.'"

— Kelly Holmes, two-time Olympic gold medalist and mental health advocate who has shared her experience with depression and self-harm[32]

I used to be a member of a Facebook group managed and owned by a business mentor and consultant who interviewed clients live inside of the group. He asked them what their business did, how they helped their clients, what their business looked like before joining his program, what their business looked like at the end of 90 days, what they believed attributed to their success, and what they did not like about his program.

I binge-watched these client interview videos, took notes, and in less than a week, I was having a sales conversation with him about one of his programs.

Success stories are one of the fastest ways to attract high-quality leads and turn them into customers. Your happy customers are a critical part of your business growth team.

HAPPY CLIENTS ARE YOUR GREATEST MARKETING ASSET

According to a Nielsen report, 68 percent of people say they trust reviews and customer opinions posted online.[33]

Before someone invests in your product or service, they want to feel confident that your solution will solve their problem and that they'll have an amazing experience. Most people will read ratings, reviews, testimonials, or case studies to help them make their decision. In fact, one study showed that online reviews impact the purchasing decision of 93 percent of consumers.

Sharing the results your customers achieve shows others what's possible.

The first time I realized the power of customer success stories was in middle school. I saw an infomercial for Tae Bo, a martial art–inspired workout, and became obsessed. I was an athlete, but I wanted visible abs. In the infomercial, I watched person after person share their experience with the program and show their before and after pictures. Everyone seemed to have six-pack abs. Even a woman as old as my grandma had visible abs.

I saved up money and bought the Tae Bo tapes online so I could do the workout I believed would leave me with six-pack abs.

The before and after case studies sealed the deal for me.

TYPES OF SOCIAL PROOF

According to the social media management company Sprout Social, social proof is the concept that people will follow the actions of the masses.[34] When a prospective customer sees that a lot of people just like them are buying a product or service and getting results, they are left thinking they should do the same.

Creating a consistent flow of social proof begins with having happy customers. Once you are consistently helping customers get results, you can focus on building a system for collecting and sharing the results your clients and customers are getting.

There are many ways to show that people like your products or services. As a business owner, it is your job to determine the best way to showcase what your offering can do for customers so they can confidently choose to buy or not.

Here are a few ways you can provide social proof.

1. Ratings and Reviews

Before my mom will see a movie in theaters, she'll look up its rating on Rotten Tomatoes. If a movie does not have a Rotten Tomato rating, my mom will not go see it in theaters. Depending on your offerings, your customers may do something similar before buying your product or service. Ratings are common for physical products, digital products such as online courses, and many service-based businesses, such as nail and hair salons, restaurants, and podcasts.

When looking at your ratings, customers use two numbers to determine if they'll invest in your product or service. The first is the average rating out of 5 or 10, depending on the scale, and the second is the total number of people who left a rating.

Having a high rating is not enough if only five people left a rating. Those five people could be your family and friends.

While there's no exact number that your company must reach in order to benefit from ratings, research shows that 3.3

out of 5 is the minimum star rating a business needs for consumers to engage[35] and 40 or more reviews are needed before consumers will consider the star rating accurate.[36]

The general rule of thumb is the higher the rating and the more people who leave a review, the better. Even a one-star increase on Yelp ratings leads to a 5 to 9 percent increase in revenue.[37]

Ratings are more effective when they are coupled with reviews. Reviews give context to a person's rating. Ideally, they succinctly share why a customer did or did not like your product or service.

A valuable review will share why the person made the purchase, if the product or service met expectations, the pros and cons, if they recommend it to others, and why or why not. The average consumer reads 10 online reviews before making a purchase decision.

Reviews are a powerful sales tool. When done well, a review can answer the following questions for your prospective customers:

- Will this work for someone like me?
- What is amazing about this product or service?
- What is not amazing about this product or service?
- Is there a solution or work-around for the things that are not great about this product or service?
- Do other people recommend this product or service?

2. Number of Sales

I remember a time when I was the only person in my family with a smartphone. By 2019, it was estimated that more than

50 percent of people with mobile devices had a smartphone.[38] Today, there are companies that help businesses capitalize on the mindset that if everyone's buying it, you should consider buying it too.

Picture this: You go to a website and are looking at an online course. While you're looking at the course, you see a pop-up every few seconds of someone else buying the course.

The software company Proof helps businesses publicly show notifications of people buying their products or services. On their website, they share that their customers see an average conversion increase of 10 percent by using this method.

3. Testimonials

The main difference between reviews and testimonials is how they are collected and displayed. Ratings and reviews are typically on a site where any customer can publicly share their experience. Testimonials, as well as case studies, are typically collected by the company.

If you are selling results, testimonials are a great way to share success stories. On average, testimonials on sales pages increase conversions by 34 percent.[39] While they are similar to reviews, testimonials typically live on your website and social media pages and you choose the best ones for display.

The most compelling testimonials specifically address the problems your customer was having before they purchased your offering, a bit about their experience, and how things look for the customer now.

Companies reach out to the customers with the best success stories for videos or written testimonials they can use to drive the sales of their products and services.

4. Case Studies

Like testimonials, case studies highlight the transformation a customer experiences through buying a product or service, but they provide the additional benefit of more detailed information and quantified results.

A social media manager may use a case study to show the specific increase in engagement, reach, and leads a client experienced from working with them.

Case studies are often written by businesses using information they've tracked and collected about their customers and often include testimonials or quotes from each customer featured in the case study.

To produce case studies, it is important to track your customer's results before, during, and after investing in your product or service.

BUILDING A SOCIAL PROOF SYSTEM

Sharing the success stories of your clients and customers can increase your revenue, but it doesn't just happen. Businesses need to create a system and a process for collecting, tracking, and stimulating social proof. This can be done in four simple steps.

Step 1: Determine the Type of Social Proof Your Prospects Want and How You'll Use It

Depending on your industry, prospective customers will naturally look for social proof on your website or on a specific review site (Yelp, Google, G2, etc.). Take the time to learn where your prospects will naturally go for customer success stories and reviews.

In episode 89 of the *Market Your Genius* podcast, I interviewed sales coach Shameca Tankerson, who advises her clients to house testimonials and case studies on one page of their website. She calls it the POW page, aka the proof of work page. This way, she can drive prospective clients to one page to hear client reviews before their sales call.

In this step, your job is to decide if your proof of work page will be on your site or a specific review site.

From there, you will need to determine which type of social proof the site needs. Is it ratings, reviews, testimonials, case studies, pop-ups highlighting recent product purchases, or a combination of these techniques?

Once you're clear on where your social proof will live and the type of social proof you need, it's time to decide how you'll use it. While some people will rely on searching for and finding reviews on their own, you can increase your leads and sales by proactively sharing your success stories. Here are some ideas:

- Read a review on your podcast then tell people where they can see more.
- Share a review, testimonial, success story, or average rating on social media and link to your POW page.
- Email case studies to prospective clients before a sales call.
- Share case studies during a webinar or speakership.
- Tell client stories in podcast interviews and highlight their results.
- Share client results in your blog posts or in a book you publish.
- Interview clients about their experience at an event, live on social media, or on your podcast.
- Share client results on your Instagram stories.

- Ask clients to share their wins in your Facebook group, and with their permission, screen grab their wins and share them online.

The key is to proactively share your social proof where your prospective customers *already* spend their time.

Get creative, and remember your social proof can be live video, prerecorded video, audio, text, or a combination.

Step 2: Decide How You'll Stimulate Reviews

After you're clear on what type of social proof you need, where it will live, and how you're going to use it, it's time to determine how you'll increase your ratings, reviews, and testimonials. Not all of your customers will leave a review, even if they loved the experience. Here are some ideas to encourage your customers to leave a rating or review.

Rewards Points or Gift Card

One of my most recent purchases was a pair of shoes. A few weeks after my purchase, I received an email from the company I bought my shoes from. The email stated that if I left a rating or a review, I'd receive rewards points that I could use for a discount on my next purchase. Other companies have offered Amazon gift cards, company gift cards, or a percentage off a future purchase. Offering rewards points or a gift card is not only a nice way to thank your customers, it's also a way to increase the likelihood that a customer will leave a rating or review that will help draw more leads to your business.

Entry into a Random Drawing Contest

Some companies cannot offer everyone a discount or a gift card. A client of mine wanted to increase reviews of their digital product. To stimulate reviews, we came up with the idea of doing a giveaway. We polled her audience to determine which prize would be most compelling then decided on a total number of winners. Then she shared with her customers that anyone who left a review by a certain date would be entered into a random drawing to win the prize. This strategy also works well for physical products and podcast reviews.

Ask Nicely

If you're just getting started, you may not have the budget to send everyone a thank-you gift, and that's okay. Many people will be willing to leave a testimonial because you took the time to ask. As a thank-you, never underestimate the power of a thank-you card.

Step 3: Identify and Reach Out to Customers

Once you're clear on how you will reward or thank people who leave a review, it's time to reach out to customers.

The first part of this step is identifying whom you would like to share their experience. If you're selling a physical or digital product, you may request a rating or review from everyone who's purchased the product. If you're requesting testimonials or looking for case study candidates, you'll have to do more research.

Reviews and Testimonials

In the last chapter, we discussed the Net Promoter Score (NPS), which is a score you give your product or service after asking customers on a scale from 1 to 10, how likely they are to refer your product or service to a friend. Many companies only actively reach out to customers who answer 9 or 10 to this question because those are the people who are extremely happy with the offering. While anyone may choose to leave a review, actively requesting reviews and testimonials from your biggest fans is a tactic that many companies use as social proof.

Case Studies

Since case studies are heavily focused on quantifiable results, companies seek customers that have had impressive results to use as case studies. If case studies are an approach you want to use, it's important to actively keep track of your customer's results before, during, and after investing in your product or service so you can identify who would be the best fit.

Step 4: Make It Simple and Easy for Your Customers

Even if the reward is a chance to win a new car, if the process for entering is too complicated, people will not take action. In this step, the goal is to have a process that makes it easy for customers to share their experience with others.

Ratings and Reviews

To make it easy for your customers to leave a rating and review, keep the process short and simple. The two easiest ways are to 1) send an email where a customer can complete the entire review process without leaving their email; 2) have them click a button to go directly to a review page where they can write a review and leave a rating.

Depending on where the ratings and reviews live, you may not be able to verify who left a rating or review without the help of your customer. If the ratings and reviews live on your website, you can easily verify who left a review based on their email address or other information.

When the rating and review lives on another website, such as Google, Yelp, or G2, you'll need the help of your customer to show you which review is theirs, especially if you are sending them a reward.

For this to work, you may ask the reviewer to use their first or last name in the review then email you a link to their review so you can verify it before sending them a reward.

The less information you need to verify a customer, the easier it will be for them to leave their honest review and receive their reward.

Testimonials

When asking customers for testimonials, you want to make it as easy as possible. To do this, I recommend asking customers to complete a short survey or questionnaire. This way your customer isn't overanalyzing what they should put in the testimonial and you can quote one or all of their answers on your testimonial page. For example, here are some questions I recommend asking your customers if you offer a program:

- What challenges or problems did you have before joining the program?
- What did you like most about the program?
- If you could change one thing about the program, what would it be?
- What results or wins did you have during this program?
- Would you recommend this program to others? If so, why?

Companies such as VideoAsk, Boast, and Magnifi allow you to easily capture video testimonials by letting customers record and submit a video from their phone after clicking a link sent via email.

Case Studies

Case studies show the transformation customers experience as a result of your product or program. Here are some ways you can make it simple for your customers to participate in a case study.

- Have customers complete a short survey at the time of purchase. Then choose a period of time after the purchase to have customers complete the same survey so you can measure their results.
- Interview customers via Restream, Zoom, StreamYard, Ecamm, or BeLive about their specific results from the program.
- Ask customers to share their wins each week in a Facebook group that you later turn into a case study guide.

Step 5: Create a Repeatable Process and Monitor Results

The final step to creating a social proof system is to create a repeatable process for collecting, tracking, and managing your social proof. This could be a checklist, a Trello board, or a Standard Operating Procedure (SOP) guide. The goal is to have a documented process for collecting, stimulating, and promoting your reviews, testimonials, and case studies.

Systems and structures allow you to repeat results.

To do this, you'll want to have one place that documents how you'll collect, manage, and share social proof. Here are some of the questions you will want your process to answer:

- How many ratings, reviews, testimonials, or case studies do you want each month, quarter, or year?
- What type of social proof does your company want (ratings, reviews, testimonials, case studies, a pop-up showcasing the number of purchases)?

- Where will your social proof live?
- How will you promote your success stories and reviews?
- From start to finish, what are the steps to collect and showcase customer success stories?
- What tools or systems will you use?
- If you're using surveys, what questions will you ask?

When you have a repeatable social proof system, it makes it easy for anyone within your company to manage it and allows you to determine where the process can be optimized or automated for success.

Take the time to identify how you will ask for, collect, and showcase client results. Here are some examples of what your social proof system could look like and how the scenarios could play out.

Ratings and Reviews

- Ten days after a customer receives your product, an email is sent asking for a rating or review.
- The email states that when the customer leaves a review, they'll receive a coupon code for $20 off their next purchase.
- A week goes by and the customer hasn't left a review.
- Another email goes out giving the customer a friendly reminder that they'll receive $20 off their next purchase if they leave a review.
- The customer clicks a button in the email that takes them to a product review page. They leave a rating and a few sentences about the product,

what they liked about it, features they wished the product had, and if they recommend the product. Then they hit SUBMIT.

- After the customer submits their review, they receive an email thanking them for leaving a review and offering a coupon code for $20 off their next purchase.
- The review and rating they submitted automatically updates on the website, adjusting the average rating.

Testimonials

- At the end of a group program, a customer receives an email with a short survey asking them on a scale from 1 to 10 how likely they are to recommend the program.
- The customer clicks nine and gives an explanation for their rating.
- The next question asks if the customer is willing to provide a testimonial for the program.
- The customer clicks yes and is asked three more questions about their experience.
- The final question asks if the information in this survey can be used as a testimonial and if the customer would like their full or partial name to be mentioned.
- The customer answers the final question and submits the survey.
- Each week a member of your team reviews the survey results and adds testimonials received to your company's proof of work page.

Case Studies

- Each week customers are asked to share their wins inside a Facebook group.
- Each week a member of your team reviews the wins and adds them to a spreadsheet.
- Each month your team reviews customer wins and identifies one to three people they believe would make great case studies.
- A member of your team reaches out to the customers identified and asks them if they'd like to do a video interview discussing their experience and results to be used as a case study to promote your company.
- The customer says yes and receives a link to schedule the interview.
- The interview is recorded.
- The full video and clips of the video interview are shared on social media, the audio of the interview is used as a podcast interview, and highlights from the interview are typed out and put into a PDF.
- The PDF and video are uploaded to a page on your company website.
- The social proof page is shared with prospective customers before a sales conversation.
- New interviews are recorded and added to your website every month.

IMPLEMENTATION CHECKLIST

The goal of this chapter is to help you showcase the results your customers have. Your proof validates your customer experience and helps prospective customers decide to buy from you (or not).

In the next chapter, we'll discuss how to create a referral system so your happy clients and strategic partners can help you attract more dream customers. But before we move on, make sure you have completed the action items from this chapter:

- ❑ Identify where your target audience will seek out reviews or testimonials about your products or services.
- ❑ On a scale of 1 to 10 (10 being highest), rate your social proof presence.
- ❑ Implement one idea you have that would increase your social proof rating by one point.
- ❑ Head to marketyourgeniusbook.com/chapter10 to see an example of a POW page, listen to the podcast interview with Shameca Tankerson, and access downloadable worksheets related to this chapter.

CHAPTER 11

BRING MORE A$$ES IN THE DOOR

"Find astonishing people and hang out with them."

— Megan Smith, third *ever* White House chief technology officer who believes in the power of collaboration and works in teams to solve big tech problems[40]

On my way to teach a workshop at a Rebelle Con conference in Richmond, Virginia, I had a fascinating conversation with my Lyft driver. Prior to moving to Virginia for retirement, he owned a barbershop in Harlem. His barbershop was so wildly successful that people paid him for advice and mentorship. Now retired, he was enjoying living in Richmond and occasionally drove for Lyft to meet interesting people. As we spoke, he shared his secrets to building a profitable business.

> I got to know our clients.
>
> If they loved drinking a certain type of soda, I always had it in the shop during their appointments.
>
> If they wanted to drink champagne while getting their haircut, I made sure I had champagne.

I treated them like kings and queens.
Then they'd ask how they could help me.
I told them to bring a friend.
It's that simple.

He then summed up his strategy with the following:

"I kissed their asses and asked them to bring more asses in the door."

REFERRAL MAGIC

My second paying client, "Jasmine," was a result of a referral from her close friend, "Krystal." Krystal knew that Jasmine was looking for a coach or consultant to help her market her business and attract quality leads. She gave Jasmine my email address and told her that I could absolutely help her with that problem and that I was amazing at what I did. She detailed how I had recently helped her with a business challenge.

I had only met Krystal twice. In fact, our second meeting was to get to know one another because we had mutual friends and were in the same town. During that second meeting, I ended up helping Krystal with her business. It turned out that Krystal implemented the strategy I had created for her during our meeting and started seeing results. This inspired her to refer Jasmine to me, and within 48 hours of speaking to Jasmine, she became my client.

There are three main reasons why I love referrals as a business growth strategy.

Reason #1: Increased Sales Conversion Rate

When a person gets on a sales call or goes to your sales page from a referral, they have a higher level of trust than other prospective customers. According to Nielsen research, people are four times more likely to buy when referred by a friend.[41]

With Jasmine, the sales call we had felt more like a formality than an inquiry. She already believed I could help her and simply wanted to know the details of my package before making a payment.

Reason #2: Shortened Sales Cycle

Depending on your business, the process of taking a prospective client from stranger to paying customer could take hours or months. In the "Just Like Dating" method we discussed earlier, the process metaphorically looks like meeting a stranger at a bar, sparking a conversation with them, exchanging numbers, messaging for a while before going on a first date, and dating for a period of time before a marriage proposal is on the table.

Referrals are similar to having a friend set you up on a date with someone they personally know, trust, and believe would be a good match for you. It shortens the time between the introduction and the proposal.

Reason #3: Lowered Customer Acquisition Costs

The marketing and sales cycle of taking someone from prospective to actual customer costs money. It could be the hourly rate of marketing yourself on social media, the cost of your time spent building strategic partnership, or the cost of sponsorship opportunities or ads. The cost of resources needed for a company to acquire new customers is called the Customer Acquisition Cost, or CAC.

According to a study by the Wharton Business School, the customer acquisition cost (CAC) for companies was $23.12 less for referrals than nonreferred customers.[42]

Referrals can have a powerful impact on the profitability of your business. The key to a quality referral is having a person directed to your business, product, or service from someone they trust.

THAT'S NOT A REFERRAL, THIS IS . . .

There are two elements that distinguish a referral from other forms of word-of-mouth marketing: (1) a person with a problem or a need is seeking a product or a service and (2) someone they trust recommends a product or service.

When I was living in Portland, Oregon, I had to fly to my hometown in New Jersey to be with my family every Christmas. One year I noticed this small, hard knot above my collarbone near my neck. I went to see my old primary care doctor, and after taking a look and running some tests, they referred me to a specialist. Based on my primary care doctor's referral, I made an appointment with the specialist. This is an example of what a referral is.

A referral exists when a person with a problem or a need—in this story, me—is sent by a person they trust—in this story, my longtime doctor—to a professional or company that can solve the problem or meet the need—in this story, the specialist.

Many doctors build the foundation of their business based on referrals from people they know and trust from medical school. When I speak to clients who say they don't have much luck with referrals, it's usually because they are using the word *referral* to describe other sources of leads. Let's dive into this concept further.

**All referrals are recommendations,
but not all recomendations are referrals.**

The Introduction Email

In the early days of my business, friends and acquaintances would connect me via email to someone they knew was starting a business. The email usually went something like this: "Nikki meet Jade, Jade meet Nikki. Nikki is an amazing business consultant, and Jade just started a business, so I figured you two should know each other."

While I greatly appreciated these emails, I quickly realized that the people I was connected to typically weren't looking for a business coach, consultant, or mentor. In fact, they didn't really understand what I did or if I could help them in the first place. One of the key components of a referral is that the person being referred to you has a problem *and* is looking to you for a solution. There needs to be a meeting of the minds. Otherwise, you might get on the phone thinking they're a potential client, and they're getting on the phone thinking they're meeting a new friend.

Introductory emails are a bit like going to the bar and speaking to a friend of your friend's partner. You might have some level of trust and familiarity with one another, but you still need to spark a conversation and decide if you want to exchange information before going on a date. This is different from being set up on a blind date.

Introductions can be helpful in building your business. They just aren't always necessarily referrals. Rather, they're touchpoints with someone who may or may not eventually become a customer.

The Affiliate Program

Another word-of-mouth marketing tactic that gets collapsed with referrals are affiliates. Affiliate marketing is when a company offers a commission to someone for promoting their product or service. The key is that you are paid for successfully marketing someone else's product or service.

The biggest distinction between an affiliate recommendation and a referral is compensation. While affiliates may believe in the product or service they are recommending, they are guaranteed a specific monetary reward for every sale made based on their recommendation.

The Shout-out

My third client came from a shout-out. A friend of mine told her Instagram and Facebook audience that I had started a business and was amazing at what I do. It just so happened that one of her friends was looking for support acquiring new customers and sent me a message. While this shout-out from a friend online led to a new client, it wasn't a referral. It was a friend spreading the word about what I do in hopes that it might help me get a lead or two.

BUILDING YOUR REFERRAL SYSTEM

So how do you get referrals?

Referrals are not a passive marketing activity. If you want referrals consistently, you will need to put a repeatable process in place.

Before you can create and implement a referral system, you must first be referable. When someone refers their network to you, they're putting their reputation on the line. Look at it this way: If a friend set you up on a blind date and you left the date thinking, *My friend doesn't know me at all, how could they set me up with that person?*, would you allow them to set you up on any more dates?

If you want clients to be referred to you, your first job is to make sure your customers have an amazing experience. This is another reason why having strong ratings, reviews, testimonials, or case studies is important to your business.

Assuming you are referable, these are the four steps to building a consistent flow of referrals for your business.

Step 1: Make Your Referral Source List

The first step to creating referrals is to identify where your referrals will come from. Typically, your referrals will come from one or more of the following four places.

Customers and Clients

Happy customers are the most popular source of referrals. When a customer sees the value in your product or service and has an amazing experience, they're more likely to tell their network about your business.

Remember the Net Promoter Score, or NPS? As a reminder, it asks one question: "On a scale from 1 to 10, how likely is it that you would recommend [insert your brand/product/service] to a friend or colleague?"

Companies that use NPS to evaluate their products or services typically only ask for a referral from those that give a rating of a 9 or 10.

Strategic Partners

Outside of customers, strategic partners are the second strongest source of referrals. These partners know what your business does, are not a competitor, and come across your ideal client in their day to day. A great way to identify strategic partners is to find people who interact with your ideal customer either before or after they work with you, just as my primary doctor was a great referral source for my specialist.

Fans

In the first year of my business, a number of clients were referred to me by people I didn't know well. They were people who saw my videos or ended up on my newsletter and heard about the results our clients received. While they were not yet ready to work with me, when people in their network were seeking support, they highly recommended me based on their experience with my content.

Family and Friends

Especially when you start your business, friends and family will be excited to help you grow your business in any way they can. Unlike customers, strategic partners, and fans, your friends and family may not know exactly what product or service you offer. This is why it's important to equip family and friends with the information they need to identify ideal referral candidates.

Step 2: Create a Referral Thank-You System

During a call with a person I met through a coaching program, we were discussing my new program and she mentioned that she might know some people who would be a good fit. I said that was great and the best way to connect us was through email or text. She then replied with, "What do I get if I send you people?" I was thrown off. I wanted to say, "A thank-you, and when I come across people, I'll send them your way if it makes sense." But I didn't know if paying referral partners was common practice. Instead, I dodged the question and suggested that she think about what she would want so we could discuss it.

This conversation made me realize that different people have different expectations when it comes to referrals. The reason I differentiate affiliates from referrals is because if someone is getting paid based on their referrals, it can change the way a referral is received. For example, if a friend uses Lyft, sends me a link to sign up for it, and we both get $5 off our next ride, I may not think twice about it. But if a doctor tells me I need to see a specialist then I find out that they get $5,000 for everyone they send to that specialist, I would question if they really thought that particular specialist was right for me or if they only referred me because they got paid.

It's your job to determine how you want to thank or reward recommendations and if your business is best suited for affiliates or referrals. For my business, we send thank-you cards to everyone who sends referrals our way, and during the holiday season, we may send candles, chocolate, or a fruit basket as a token of our appreciation for their support.

When it comes to thanking your referral sources, it's important to act in alignment with what feels right for your company.

Step 3: Build Relationships

Once you know where your referrals can come from and how you're going to reward referrals, it's time to start building relationships with those who can refer customers to your business.

If you want more customers, build more relationships.

As we discussed, when someone is referring their network to you, they are putting their reputation on the line. Referrals are all about trust; that's why relationship building is crucial to the referral process.

Get to know your referral sources. If they're not a customer or a friend, take time to meet them in person or virtually. Get to know who their target customers are and who is in their network. If they are a business owner and potential strategic partner, discover how they help their customers and what their customers typically need before or after working with them. Finally evaluate if you get along or vibe.

Once you start getting to know people, you can decide if they'd be a good referral partner or not.

There's a debate on if you should or shouldn't ask your network for referrals. Some people believe that to get referrals, you should ask. In fact, when I first started my business, I joined Business Network International (BNI) for a year. The idea behind BNI is to meet with the same group of business owners every week to build a referral network. Each week you'd share with the members what types of referrals you were looking for and ask for the referral.

There is also an argument that you shouldn't ask for referrals and instead consistently thank the people who naturally refer business your way. There's an art and a science to referrals. If you've tried the strategy of not asking for referrals and it's working for you, keep it up. If it isn't working, try another approach.

Step 4: Design a Repeatable Process for Stimulating Referrals and Track the Results

Once you've successfully received referrals, write down the steps you took to receive each one. What did you learn from the process? How could you improve the process? When you take the time to write down the steps you took, you can create a repeatable process.

You can implement the M.A.A.D. Scientist Method we discussed earlier in Chapter 8 to build a referral system that consistently generates leads.

Here's an example of a referral system for nutritionists.

- Reach out to personal trainers in your area.
- Invite them to coffee or tea to learn more about their clients and their business and discuss the results your clients get from your role as a nutritionist.
- Send a follow-up email or note saying it was great to meet them.
- After a few weeks, follow up by sending information they can use to help their clients get stronger results.
- Follow up to understand if the information you sent them was valuable. If so, send them a relevant article or podcast episode.
- After each referral, send them a thank-you note.
- At the end of the year, send a thank-you gift as a token of your appreciation.
- Throughout the year, keep track of all the people you've connected with, how the relationships have developed, and who became strong referral partners. Based on this information, adjust your plan as necessary.

IMPLEMENTATION CHECKLIST

The goal of this chapter is to help you start generating referrals for your business. In the next chapter, we'll discuss creating systems and structures so your dream customers continue to buy from you. Before heading to the next chapter, make sure you complete the following action items:

- ❑ Create a list of everyone who has referred customers to your business.
- ❑ List all of your current and past customers.
- ❑ List the top 20-plus businesses that could become strong referral sources for your business.
- ❑ Start connecting with people on your list.
- ❑ Head to marketyourgeniusbook.com/chapter11 to access referral templates.

CHAPTER 12

CLIENTS 4 LIFE

"Never limit yourself because of others' limited imagination; never limit others because of your own limited imagination."

— Mae Jemison, the first African American woman to travel in space. Mae became an astronaut after attending Stanford at the age of 16, attending Cornell University Medical College, and working in the Peace Corps as a medical officer.[43]

"Hi, Nikki. I know we only have a few sessions left, and I just wanted to know how I renew and if we can keep our same call time?"

At the time my client said this to me, the longest I had worked with anyone was 90 days. I had it in my mind that you work with your consultant, coach, or mentor for the terms of your agreement then go on your merry way. When my client asked what the next steps were to continue working together, I realized that I needed to reconsider this belief.

"You can absolutely keep your same time," I replied. "Let's schedule a short call either this week or next week to specifically discuss how we can continue to work together and realign on your goals."

When we got off Zoom, I sat down and thought about what it would be like if I worked with all my clients for more than 90 days.

THE LIFETIME VALUE OF A CUSTOMER

Warning: The following section includes math to illustrate key points. My goal is to make it as easy to follow as possible, even for those who hate math.

As I imagined what it would be like to work with clients for longer than 90 days, I started to envision the benefits for our clients and for my business.

I began to visualize all of the things I could help them achieve as we continued to work together that I couldn't do within a shorter time frame. Then I started looking at how it could impact my business.

Acquiring new customers is important but so is keeping the ones you already have.

When I worked in the start-up world, Customer Lifetime Value (CLV or CLTV) was a metric we often reviewed. The Customer Lifetime Value is the average amount a person will spend with your business for as long as they're a customer minus the amount you spent in marketing to acquire that customer, the goal being to increase the CLV over time to increase profit. Increasing your profitability with existing customers who already know you is typically easier and faster than acquiring new ones.

There are two primary adjustments you can make to increase your Customer Lifetime Value: 1) You can work with customers for a longer period of time, or 2) you can increase your prices.

To give you a simple example, let's say that the average amount of time a customer will buy from you is three months. Let's also say that your customers spend, on average, $1,000 per month with your business. If you spend, on average, $500 to acquire each customer, your CLV is $2,500.

Customer's Monthly Spend*	**$1,000**
Customer Lifetime*	**X 3 months**
Customer's Lifetime Spend*	**$3,000**
Customer's Lifetime Spend	**$3,000**
Cost to Acquire Customer*	**–$500**
Customer Lifetime Value	**$2,500**

* Since this amount varies from customer to customer, take the average.

If your average customer lifetime was 12 months instead of three, your customer lifetime value would be $11,500.

Customer's Monthly Spend*	**$1,000**	**$1,000**
Customer Lifetime*	**X 3 months**	**X 12 months**
Customer's Lifetime Spend*	**$3,000**	**$12,000**
Customer's Lifetime Spend	**$3,000**	**$12,000**
Cost to Acquire Customer*	**–$500**	**–$500**
Customer Lifetime Value	**$2,500**	**$11,500**

The longer your clients stay with you, the larger the lifetime value.

Now let's say that instead of increasing time, you increase the average monthly spending. In this example, the average amount of time a customer will buy from you is three months, but your customers spend, on average, $2,000 per month with your business. If you spend, on average, $500 to acquire each customer, your CLV is $5,500.

Customer's Monthly Spend*	$1,000	$2,000
Customer Lifetime*	X 3 months	X 3 months
Customer's Lifetime Spend*	$3,000	$6,000
Customer's Lifetime Spend	$3,000	$6,000
Cost to Acquire Customer*	–$500	–$500
Customer Lifetime Value*	$2,500	$5,500

The higher your average customer spending is, the larger the lifetime value.

Since you will likely increase your prices over time, the bulk of this chapter will focus on how to increase the average amount of time your customers will buy from you.

MAKING IT A WIN-WIN

Customers don't stay with you just for the heck of it. They stay because of the value. Think about a product that has earned your loyalty. Maybe it's the products you use on your hair or your skin. Maybe it's the brand of jeans you buy. Maybe it's a car manufacturer. Think of something you continue to purchase and ask yourself why.

Then ask yourself, *Why would someone remain a customer of my business?*

As I started to answer this question for my own business, I started thinking about what a three-, four-, or five-year relationship could look like.

I envisioned the stages of business they'd reach, the milestones they'd hit, the goals they could achieve. I stopped thinking solely about short-term transactions and started thinking about the potential for long-term customer relationships.

Here are some reasons your customers may remain brand loyal:

- You've helped them get results and they believe they can achieve their next goals with you.
- You offer a superior experience than your competitors.
- They feel like you're a true partner and have their back.
- Your customer service is amazing.
- You know what they need or want next before they do, and you always have it available for them.
- You know their history and they trust that you customize support based on their history.

I encourage you to create your own list of reasons customers would continue to buy from you past their first purchase. If you already have customers that have continued to purchase from you, take the time to ask them why, then add their reasons to your list.

SETTING EXPECTATIONS

You may be thinking, *I get it already! Having customers for a longer time can be a win-win for everyone, but I can't ask a client to sign a five-year agreement.*

Know that I completely get it. In fact, the longest commitment currently offered to our clients is 12 months. But that doesn't mean I don't seed the idea of working together longer. Here's what I mean: When a customer comes to you, they're typically looking for a specific solution. If you're selling face wash, maybe that goal is to get rid of acne. If you're selling health coaching, maybe it's to lose weight. And if you're a marketing agency, maybe it's to get more leads.

At the beginning of the relationship, you want to sell people what they want and deliver on that offer.

Building a long-term relationship with clients requires both parties to see the possibility of a future together.

One of the main reasons people remain loyal is because your business has helped them achieve a desired result.

Let's take a look at some examples and explore what it would look like to sell a customer the short-term result and seed the benefits of remaining a long-term customer.

Skincare Example

Let's say you have a skincare product that helps people get rid of their acne in 30 days.

When marketing the product, you showcase studies of people who used the product for 30 days and saw their acne go away. Then you share that people who used the product for six months to a year also saw their acne-related scarring go away as well.

If a customer has acne, they may say, "Great, I'm going to buy this product and it will solve my acne problem, and when I continue to use it, it will also get rid of my scars." At the time of purchase, the customer is already open to the idea of using this product for six months to a year.

If you deliver on the promise of getting rid of their acne, they are more likely to continue using the product to help reduce their scarring.

In this example, the idea of a long-term customer relationship was shared early by selling potential customers on their immediate need and painting a picture of a long-term relationship.

Weight-Loss Example

If you're a personal trainer, you may say something like, "In the first four to six months, I'll help you reach your goal of losing 15 to 20 pounds. Once you hit your weight goal, if we continue to work together for the rest of the year, we'll focus on losing inches and defining your muscles since I know you have a goal of defining your back muscles before you walk down the aisle in your wedding dress."

Again, the immediate need or want is your focus while also painting a picture of a longer-term relationship if it's in alignment with the customer's goals.

Marketing Agency Example

Let's pretend you own a marketing agency. When speaking to a client who is interested in increasing their leads, you may say something like, "In six months, our customers see 25 percent growth in their leads by optimizing the website traffic they already have. When we work together, we'll spend six months testing, validating, and implementing the strategy so you can see an increase in leads with the traffic you're currently getting to your site. Then, if we continue to work together, we'll create and validate ads to increase your site traffic."

When you seed a long-term relationship, you're telling prospective customers what they can expect in the short term and what's possible in the long term.

BUILDING A CLIENTS 4 LIFE SYSTEM

So how do you build a game plan for long-term customers? If you're serious about retaining customers, take the time to identify how a long-term relationship could be a win-win for both parties. The Clients 4 Life System is a four-step process that helps you get clear on what a long-term customer relationship could look like and how you can start communicating the possibility with prospective customers. Let's walk through the Clients 4 Life System.

Step 1: Picture the Ideal Long-Term Relationship with a Customer

Remember the dream customer testimonial that we discussed earlier? You were tasked with writing the testimonial you would like to receive from customers then using that dream testimonial to create a program worthy of such praise.

Building your Clients 4 Life System begins with a similar exercise. Write down the dream case studies you would like to have from customers who have purchased from you for 3, 5, or 10 years. What results have they achieved in that time frame? Why have they remained a customer year after year?

Creating a long-term relationship with customers begins with understanding the long-term value you can deliver.

Step 2: Identify the Notable Milestones Along the Journey

When I do long-term planning with clients, we start with where they want to be in 10 years. The long-term vision shows you directionally where they want to be in the future. Then we think about what they want to accomplish in the next year and the next three years. While most people cannot create a detailed 10-year plan for their life, they can set short-term goals that are in alignment with their long-term vision.

You want to do the same thing. Once you've identified the results your long-term customers want to achieve, work backward and identify what milestones they need to focus on that could help make their vision a reality.

Let's say that in 10 years, your client wants to reach $25M in revenue for their business. Together, you may set a goal to reach $1M in three years and to create consistent revenue within the first 12 months.

Complete this exercise for your dream customer. Identify where they likely want to be in the long-term then identify 12-month and three-year milestones that are in alignment with that vision.

Step 3: Create a Road Map for Your Customers

Your customers are looking for you to point them in the right direction. They know where they want to go, but they may not know how to get there.

In this step, you'll outline the pathway for taking your clients from point A to their final destination.

Map out the activities your customers will need to complete between each milestone. If you help customers build profitable businesses, in the first 12 months, you may have your customer focus on validating their business idea, building their strategic plan, and testing their marketing strategy.

In the next couple of years, they may focus on increasing their sales and profitability or building their team.

In this step, you want to create a plan for your clients to reach their 12-month and three-year milestones and have a general idea of what else it will take for them to achieve their big vision.

Step 4: Communicate the Road Map with Prospective Customers

Finally, you'll want to communicate to your prospective customers that you have a road map for them that extends beyond their immediate need.

An effective way to do this is to create a signature system, framework, or three- to seven-stage process. Essentially you want to show your prospective customers that you have an easy-to-follow process for them to reach their goals. For example, in 1983, Neil C. Churchill and Virginia L. Lewis published an article in the *Harvard Business Review* called "The Five Stages of Small Business Growth."[44] If Churchill and Lewis were marketing a business consulting company to prospective clients, they could address all five stages in their marketing. This would allow prospective clients to identify which stage they were at then recognize that getting to stage 5 would require a long-term relationship with Churchill and Lewis.

Take the time to map out how you would help customers in a long-term relationship. Depending on your business, a long-term relationship could be a year or 10 years. Think about everything your customers would need to accomplish in order to achieve their long-term vision. Ask yourself how you can group these steps into three to seven major moves. When you can break down the journey to accomplishing a goal into a few steps, it makes it easier for a prospective client to see their goal as achievable. Then you can communicate which step or steps could be accomplished in the short-term and which could be accomplished in a long-term relationship.

A CLIENTS 4 LIFE SYSTEM METAPHOR

Pretend your friend wants to go on a road trip with you over 2,700 miles, from Philadelphia, Pennsylvania, to Los Angeles, California. You agree to help plan the trip and start by identifying the tourist attractions and necessary pit stops you'll take along the way. You look at a map and identify the specific roads and highways that will get you where you want to go. Now that you have a plan, you communicate all of this to your friend to see if they're in agreement.

This is just like the Clients 4 Life System. In Step 1, you get clear on the vision. In this story, the vision is driving from Philly to LA. In Step 2, you identify milestones that are in alignment with your vision. In this story, you identify the tourist attractions and necessary pit stops between Philadelphia and Los Angeles. In Step 3, you create a road map for your customers to realize their vision. This is depicted in the story by the roads and highways you choose to create your road map. Finally, you communicate the plan with prospective customers to see if they're in alignment with the process. If they are, then you move forward. If there are questions or concerns, there may still be work to do, but this is the process you want to follow. And if it's not in alignment at all, then you'll be able to avoid a long road trip with a friend who has a different definition of the word *vacation* than you do.

Creating a Clients 4 Life System is no different than creating a travel plan from Philadelphia to Los Angeles. Focus on the ultimate destination and plan for important milestones along the way.

IMPLEMENTATION CHECKLIST

The goal of this chapter is for you to build a lasting relationship with your customers. Make sure you implement the lessons from this chapter with these action items:

- ❑ Calculate your current CLV.
- ❑ Brainstorm ways you can increase your CLV.
- ❑ Build your Clients 4 Life System.
- ❑ Head to marketyourgeniusbook.com/chapter12 to see examples of the Clients 4 Life System, download worksheets, and access a CLV calculator.

CONCLUSION

"Impossible is not a fact; it's an attitude."

— Christiana Figueres,[45] Costa Rican diplomat, anthropologist, and climate change champion who was a "force of nature" behind the history-making Paris Agreement to combat climate change[46]

Early in my business, I joined Brendon Burchard's High Performance Academy. In one of the training modules, Burchard states that he should be able to tell what someone's goals are by looking at their calendar. At the time, my goal was to write my first book, a dream that had been on my resolutions list since I was a kid. Every year, I had a reason for not accomplishing my goal: "I have to wait until I have more experience." "I don't know what I would write about." "I'm not sure how to get a book deal." "I don't know how to self-publish." The list of excuses was a mile long. But Burchard's video struck a chord that broke through decades of excuses. I kept having the thought, *If you don't start putting time on your calendar to work on your book, it's never going to happen.*

I stopped watching the video and started researching how to get a book deal. I asked everyone I knew if they had a published author in their network and asked for a connection so I could ask them questions. I found workshops about how to write and publish a book, and signed up. Once I learned something new, I took an action step. All of my baby steps led to Reid Tracy, CEO of Hay House, calling me to say that my book was being published. I'm often asked what I did to make this happen, but the truth is the exact steps I took are not as important as the principles that led to the achievement. Focus, action, patience, and resilience are the reasons I accomplished my goal. Not every step I took was successful, but I remained focused on my goal, I kept taking action, I remained patient, and I never gave up.

These same principals will help you achieve your goals. You've now learned the frameworks to get started, but the only way to know exactly what's going to work for your business is to get into action and work through the challenges.

WHAT TO PUT ON YOUR CALENDAR

In this book, we've covered how to attract, acquire, and retain customers for your business. The content in this book can be broken down into the following 10 action steps:

1. Determine where you want your business to go and identify where you are now so you know what to plug into your metaphorical GPS.
2. Identify your superpowers and choose what you want to be known for in the marketplace so you can differentiate your brand from the competition.
3. Get clear on the problem your business solves and who wants to invest in a solution to that problem right now.
4. Validate your business by creating and offering a minimum viable solution for the problem you will solve.
5. Once you know there's demand for your offer, create a sales and marketing plan to attract your target audience, generate leads, and turn cold leads into happy customers.
6. Test and validate that plan like a scientist.
7. Deliver an amazing experience to your customers and track their results.
8. Request testimonials, collect reviews, or create case studies for social proof.

9. Create a referral system for another source of customers.
10. Increase your revenue by increasing the average length of the relationship you have with your customers and their average lifetime value.

The key to having this plan work for you is to implement what you've learned. Put time in your calendar to complete the exercises in this book. A full checklist and complimentary videos can be found in the companion course at marketyourgeniusbook.com/implementation.

REVISITING THE INNER SOUNDTRACK REMIX

Overall, we have primarily talked about strategy and action. But I can't end this book without mentioning the power your thoughts have over your actions. Could I have started a business when I originally wanted to? Absolutely. Could I have written a book when the idea first crossed my mind? Definitely! But I didn't because of the thoughts playing in my head. On a soundtrack, some songs may make you want to dance while others will make you want to cry. The same is true for the inner soundtrack playing in your head, only the music is a sequence of thoughts. There are even times when you metaphorically have a song you can't stand stuck in your head; only instead of it just being annoying, it's also disempowering.

My inner soundtrack repeated things, like "You're not good enough," "What if you fail?" "People will judge you," "Who do you think you are?" and the list goes on. I allowed myself to believe those thoughts, and as a result, I stopped myself from going after what I truly wanted.

We all have these thoughts. They are not innately good or bad; they are just thoughts. If your thoughts don't help you move toward your goal and you take them at face value, your dreams usually end up in either the "maybe one day if I'm lucky" or the "wouldn't that be nice" pile.

As you take action, pay attention to when you procrastinate or resist moving forward. Pay attention to the thoughts, beliefs, or fears that come up. And if it feels right to you, get support in addressing that resistance.

There are entire books, seminars, courses, retreats, and programs designed to help people reprogram, rewire, or change their thoughts. At the end of this book's free companion course, you'll find a list of resources that have helped me. I encourage you to seek out the resources that resonate with you.

You are 100 percent capable of creating a business you're *MADLY* in love with. You just have to believe it's possible.

Remember, you got this!

ENDNOTES

Preface

1. *Oxford English Mini Dictionary, 8th Edition* (United Kingdom: Oxford University Press, 2013).

Chapter 1

2. Quotabelle, *Grit & Grace: Uncommon Wisdom for Inspiring Leaders Designed to Make You Think* (New York: Rock Point, 2018), 102–103.

3. Sean Covey, *The 7 Habits of Highly Effective Teens: The Ultimate Teenage Success Guide* (New York: Simon & Schuster, 2011).

4. International Coaching Federation (ICF), *2016 ICF Global Coaching Study: Executive Summary,* 2016, https://coachingfederation.org/app/uploads/2017/12/2016ICFGlobalCoachingStudy_ExecutiveSummary-2.pdf.

5. "Billy Horschel on Mental Toughness," *Game Changers with Molly Fletcher,* April 25, 2017. https://www.youtube.com/watch?v=U-Rsi3e3TN0.

Chapter 2

6. Stephanie Krikorian, "How an Apple Cake Saved This Woman's Home," *O, The Oprah Magazine,* June 2014, https://www.oprah.com/spiritangela-logan-mortgage-apple-cakes-becoming-an-entrepreneur.

Chapter 3

7. Quotabelle, *Grit & Grace,* 32–33.

8. CB Insights, "The Top 20 Reasons Startups Fail," November 6, 2019, https://www.cbinsights.com/research/startup-failure-reasons-top/.

9. KISSmetrics, "Calculating Lifetime Value Infographic," https://blog.kissmetrics.com/wp-content/uploads/2011/08/calculating-ltv.pdf.

10. Allie Townsend, "All-Time 100 Greatest Toys," *Time,* February 16, 2011, http://content.time.com/time/specials/packages/article/0,28804,2049243_2048654_2049146,00.html.

11. W. Chan Kim and Renée Mauborgne, *Blue Ocean Strategy: How to Create Uncontested Market Space and Make the Competition Irrelevant* (Boston: Harvard Business Review Press, 2015).

12. Seth Godin, "In Search of the Minimum Viable Audience," *Seth's Blog*, July 12, 2017, https://seths.blog/2017/07/in-search-of-the-minimum-viable-audience/.

Chapter 4

13. Quotabelle, *Grit & Grace*, 104–105.

14. Napoleon Hill, *Think and Grow Rich* (New York: Jeremy P. Tarcher/Penguin, 2005), 22–23.

15. Corporate Finance Institute, "What Is a Profit Margin?" https://corporatefinanceinstitute.com.

Chapter 5

16. Quotabelle, *Grit & Grace*, 128–129.

17. Arlisha R. Norwood, "Maria Tallchief," National Women's History Museum (NWHM), https://www.womenshistory.org/education-resources/biographies/maria-tallchief.

Chapter 6

18. Quotabelle, *Grit & Grace*, 78–79.

19. Jessica Jackley, "About," http://www.jessicajackley.com/about.

20. Content Marketing Institute, "What Is Content Marketing?" https://contentmarketinginstitute.com/what-is-content-marketing/.

Chapter 7

21. Kimothy Joy, *That's What She Said: Wise Words from Influential Women* (New York: HarperCollins, 2018), 62–63.

22. Omar, "Webinar Marketing for Coaches: Your Playbook," WebinarNinja, February 28, 2020, https://webinarninja.com/webinar-marketing-for-coaches-your-playbook/.

Chapter 8

23. Kimothy Joy, *That's What She Said*, 8–9.

24. Mithu Storoni, "The Real Reason Why Your Brain Is So Scared of Failure," Inc., March 7, 2018, https://www.inc.com/mithu-storoni/your-brain-isnt-afraid-of-failure-heres-whats-really-going-on.html.

25. History.com, "Who Really Invented the Light Bulb?" https://www.history.com/topics/inventions/ask-history-who-really-invented-the-light-bulb-video.

26. Thomas A. Edison Papers, Rutgers University, http://edison.rutgers.edu.

27. Francis Robbins Upton, letter to Thomas Edison, June 19,1884, Thomas A. Edison Papers, Rutgers University, http://edison.rutgers.edu/NamesSearch/SingleDoc.php?DocId=D8429ZAO.

Chapter 9

28. Blake Morgan, "50 Stats That Prove the Value of Customer Experience," *Forbes*, September 24,2019, https://www.forbes.com/sites/blakemorgan/2019/09/24/50-stats-that-prove-the-value-of-customer-experience/?sh=41a6495a4ef2.

29. NICE Satmetrix, "What Is Net Promoter?" https://www.netpromoter.com/know/.

30. NET Promoter System, "Measuring Your NET Promoter Score," https://www.netpromotersystem.com/about/measuring-your-net-promoter-score/.

31. NET Promoter System, "How the NET Promoter Score Relates to Growth," https://www.netpromotersystem.com/about/how-net-promoter-score-relates-to-growth/.

Chapter 10

32. Quotabelle, *Grit & Grace*, 76–77.

33. The Nielsen Company, *Global Trust in Advertising and Brand Messages*, September 2013, https://www.nielsen.com/wp-content/uploads/sites/3/2019/04/Nielsen-Global-Trust-in-Advertising-Report-September-2013.pdf.

34. Dominique Jackson, "Social Proof: How to Use Marketing Psychology to Boost Conversions," Sprout Social, May 29, 2018, https://sproutsocial.com/insights/social-proof/.

35. Podium, "State of Online Reviews," https://www.podium.com/resources/podium-state-of-online-reviews/#:~:text=Key%20Findings%3A,business%20consumers%20would%20engage%20with.

36. Coral Ouellette, "Social Proof Statistics: Powerful Facts That Will Help You Boost Your Brand," OptinMonster, October 7, 2019, https://optinmonster.com/social-proof-statistics/#:~:text=Social%20Proof%20Statistics%3A%20Building%20

Trust&text=88%25%20of%20consumers%20trust%20user,family%20before%20making%20a%20purchase.&text=70%25%20of%20people%20will%20trust,they%20don't%20even%20know.

37. *Harvard Magazine*, "HBS Study Finds Positive Yelp Reviews Lead to Increased Business," October 5, 2011, https://harvardmagazine.com/2011/10/hbs-study-finds-positive-yelp-reviews-lead-to-increased-business#:~:text=HBS%20Study%20Finds%20Positive%20Yelp%20Reviews%20Boost%20Business&text=a%20one%2Dstar%20increase%20in,restaurants%20with%20chain%20affiliation%2C%20and.

38. Laura Silver, "Smartphone Ownership Is Growing Rapidly around the World, but Not Always Equally," PEW Research Center, February 5, 2019, https://www.pewresearch.org/global/2019/02/05/smartphone-ownership-is-growing-rapidly-around-the-world-but-not-always-equally/.

39. Coral Ouellette, "Social Proof Statistics," October 7, 2019.

Chapter 11

40. Quotabelle, *Grit & Grace*, 74–75.

41. Nielsen, "Under the Influence: Consumer Trust in Advertising," September 17, 2013, https://www.nielsen.com/us/en/insights/article/2013/under-the-influence-consumer-trust-in-advertising/.

42. Philipp Schmitt, Bernd Skiera, and Christophe Van den Bulte, *Referral Programs and Customer Value*, January 2011, https://faculty.wharton.upenn.edu/wp-content/uploads/2012/04/Schmitt-Skiera-vandenBulte-2011-Referral-Programs-Customer-Value.pdf.

Chapter 12

43. Kimothy Joy, *That's What She Said*, 66–67.

44. Neil C. Churchill and Virginia L. Lewis, "The Five Stages of Small Business Growth," *Harvard Business Review*, May 1983, https://hbr.org/1983/05/the-five-stages-of-small-business-growth.

Conclusion

45. Quotabelle, *Grit & Grace*, 172–173.

46. United Nations Climate Change, "The Paris Agreement," https://unfccc.int/process-and-meetings/the-paris-agreement/the-paris-agreement.

ACKNOWLEDGMENTS

The creation of this book would not have been possible without the contribution and encouragement of so many. I am truly filled with joy and gratitude for those that helped me create this book and those who took the time to read it. Writing a book and building a business are not solo journeys. So to all whom I have met along my path, thank you. Since I could fill up an entire book sharing my gratitude for all those who impacted my journey, the following gives a shout-out to a few individuals and communities.

Thank you to Maria, my closest friend, for your love, support, and real talk during the emotional roller-coaster of writing and publishing this book. Thank you for reminding me that I'm "more than enough" on days that I forgot. Thank you to my parents and sister for listening to my long-winded stories about this process and being excited for me even if you weren't 100 percent clear on what I was saying. Thank you for grabbing groceries and even doing some of my laundry on days when I isolated myself to work on the manuscript. Thank you to Amanda, Haley, Keenah, Megan, Margy, Naketa, Emily, Sandra, and Annie for your friendship and encouragement throughout the process.

To the amazing community of women who read the earliest version of this book, thank you for helping me stay accountable and write a book I am proud of.

Thank you to my amazing editor Lisa Cheng for helping me make this book even better than my initial manuscript. Your suggestions, edits, and encouragement were priceless. Thank you to Patty Gift and the editorial team at Hay House for believing in my book concept and helping to make my author dreams a reality. Thank you to Reid Tracy for your mentorship and for support sharing my message with the world. I can't thank you enough!

Tricia Breidenthal, Yvette Granados, and Kathleen Lynch, thank you for creating an amazing cover, and thank you to Julie Davison for the interior design. Thank you to Steve Morris, Michelle Ayala, Carrie Wellbaum, and Guido Diaz for helping me produce the audiobook. Thank you to Lindsay McGinty, Sierra Hernandez, Catherine Rollins, Marlene Robinson, Stacey Smith, Diane Thomas, Anna Pettit, and all members of the Hay House family that helped me get this book in the hands of more people.

To my friends at Interview Connections, thank you for helping me reach more people with my stories. To my amazing team, thank you for helping me create a business that helps others each and every day. A special thank you to Selene Diaz for keeping me organized and sane.

Thank you to Niyc Pidgeon for your support as I wrote my book proposal. Thank you, Linda Sivertsen and Danielle La Porte, for creating content and materials that helped me write the proposal that made this book possible. Thank you to Brendon Burchard for creating High Performance Academy, which gave me the kick in the butt I needed to stop delaying my book dreams and start taking consistent action.

To all my mentors, past and present, thank you for your guidance and support. Every experience has shaped who I am today. A special thank-you to my current and past clients. Thank you for showing up. Thank you for doing the work. And thank you for allowing me to share your experiences within the pages of this book so they can help others.

Thank you to all my friends and loved ones for your love, messages, and kind words. Having you in my life brings me immense joy. Thank you to the Universe for showing me that anything is possible.

To my loved ones Auntie Anita, Grandma Ruby, Grandma Helen, and Pop Pop, I will always wish for more time and am forever grateful for the impact you've made in my life.

ABOUT THE AUTHOR

Nikki Nash is an international speaker and marketing mentor for women entrepreneurs. As host of the *Market Your Genius* podcast and founder of the Genius Profit Society, she equips entrepreneurs and authors with the tools and resources they need to share and profit from their experiences.

Known for empowering people to quit making excuses and start going after their dreams, Nikki uses her extensive business and personal development background to help women create a business and a life they're MADLY in love with.

Prior to entrepreneurship, Nikki served as a lead marketing instructor for General Assembly; head of marketing at tech start-up Rest Devices; senior marketing manager at Intel Corporation, where she won the Marketing Excellence Award; brand management MBA intern at The Coca-Cola Company; and media planner and buyer at advertising agency Publicis Worldwide on the Kraft Foods account. She has also worked for brands such as InStyle, Travel + Leisure, and Louis Vuitton MOËT Hennessy. Learn more at nikkinash.co.

Listen to the podcast: marketyourgenius.co
Connect with Nikki on Instagram: @nikkinashofficial

Hay House Titles of Related Interest

THE SHIFT, the movie,
starring Dr. Wayne W. Dyer
(available as a 1-DVD program, an expanded 2-DVD set,
and an online streaming video)
Learn more at www.hayhouse.com/the-shift-movie

***

HIGH PERFORMANCE HABITS: How Extraordinary People Become That Way, by Brendon Burchard

MEANT FOR MORE: The Proven Formula to Turn Your Knowledge into Profits, by Lisa Sasevich

MOVE THE NEEDLE: Yarns from an Unlikely Entrepreneur, by Shelly Brander

PURPOSE: Find Your Truth and Embrace Your Calling, by Jessica Huie

RISK FORWARD: Embrace the Unknown and Unlock Your Hidden Genius, by Victoria Labalme

SHE MEANS BUSINESS: Turn Your Ideas into Reality and Become a Wildly Successful Entrepreneur, by Carrie Green

All of the above are available at your local
bookstore or may be ordered by visiting:

Hay House USA: www.hayhouse.com®
Hay House Australia: www.hayhouse.com.au
Hay House UK: www.hayhouse.co.uk
Hay House India: www.hayhouse.co.in

***